This People,
This Parish

Other Books by Robert K. Hudnut

Surprised by God: What It Means to Be a Minister in Middle-Class America Today

An Active Man and the Christ

A Sensitive Man and the Christ

A Thinking Man and the Christ

The Sleeping Giant: Arousing Church Power in America

Arousing the Sleeping Giant: How to Organize Your Church for Action

Church Growth Is Not the Point

The Bootstrap Fallacy: What the Self-Help Books Don't Tell You

This People, This Parish

ROBERT K. HUDNUT

Ministry Resources Library

Zondervan Publishing House • Grand Rapids, MI

THIS PEOPLE, THIS PARISH

Copyright © 1986 by
Robert K. Hudnut

MINISTRY RESOURCES LIBRARY
is an imprint of
Zondervan Publishing House
1415 Lake Drive S.E.
Grand Rapids, Michigan 49506

Library of Congress Cataloging in Publication Data

Hudnut, Robert K.
      This people, this parish

            1. Church.   2. Pastoral theology.   3. Christian life—
            Presbyterian authors.   4. Hudnut, Robert K.   I. Title.

BV600.2.H84   1986   253   85–29625

ISBN   0–310–38241–6

Edited by Michael G. Smith

Designed by Louise Bauer

Printed in the United States of America

86   87   88   89   90   91   /   10   9   8   7   6   5   4   3   2   1

For
  Heidi, Rob, Heather, and Matt

And with gratitude to the beloved communities of
  Westminster Presbyterian Church, Albany, New York
  St. Luke Presbyterian Church, Wayzata, Minnesota
  Winnetka Presbyterian Church, Winnetka, Illinois

Contents

Where two or three are gathered
in my name, there am I in the
midst of them.

Matthew 18:20

Preface

This is a love story—of pastor for people, people for pastor, both for God, and God for both.

It has its pain as well as its joy. What love story hasn't? If there is no pain, there is no love. We hurt a lot when we love a lot.

But the dominant theme of this love story is joy. "That my joy may be in you," Jesus said, "and your joy be made full." Here are plain, average, ordinary people living out their lives together and in so doing finding joy.

It is in the "together" that they find the joy. For they are being the church together. "Where two or three are gathered in my name," Jesus said, "there am I in the midst of them." They have found joy because they have found Christ—through one another.

The particular churches reflected in these pages are by no means put forward as ideal. They are simply a composite of the three parishes I have served, called together by God at particular places and times, and presented here, warts and all.

If the experience of these people in these parishes can be helpful to other people in other parishes, I will be grateful. If not, I am sure there are other ways to be drawn to Christ. Nevertheless, the way of the local church is one way, and a good one, which has worked for centuries to bring people to Jesus.

It is now twenty-five years since I was ordained. This book is a sequel of sorts to my first book, *Surprised by God: What It Means to Be a Minister in Middle-Class America Today,* written eight years after becoming a pastor. As in that book, the people portrayed here are real people and the events actual events. I have, however, tried to protect anonymity. My intent is to use the particular to suggest the universal rather than to use the particular to dwell on it or to identify the person involved. Wherever the recounting of an event might be perceived as appearing to breach a confidence, permission was received from the church member involved.

I am indebted to the late naturalist Hal Borland for the title. His book *This Hill, This Valley* moved me deeply. One day after reading it I appeared on his doorstep. He wasn't there, but his wife and dog entertained my wife and me and our little girl.

I am also indebted to Fern Erickson, former church secretary, who turned my disheveled pages into luminous type.

Finally, I am grateful to the people of the parishes I have served for asking me to share in the joys and sorrows of their lives and for their willingness, in turn, to share mine.

Chapter 1

God in This Parish

More

I come and go across the face of this parish. One morning a baby is born. Two mornings later a woman dies. A couple comes to get married. A man goes to the hospital for tests. A woman describes the death of her child. A young woman graduates at the head of her class. A man is on his way to becoming president of a great corporation. Another man loses his job.

It is the ebb and flow of our life together. This people, this parish is like a great sea heaving, the tides strong and the currents swift. In every home, as I go down the street tonight, some frail craft is plying that sea between sorrow and joy. The doors open, and I am asked in.

Can it be that people invite the pastor in because they want to share their laughter and their tears? I think so. But there is more to it than that. They invite the pastor because at times like these they long for the transcendent. They yearn for something more in their lives. It is that yearning for something more that we call religion.

This is not to say that life without God cannot be good. It is only to say that life with God can be better. At least it is more. It brings a dimension that otherwise one would not have.

The reason doors open to pastors is that people want to live full lives. They are not content with plying the Atlantic. They want the Pacific, too.

Images

Her older brother was killed by her father. He fell off the back of the car as his father was backing up. "Oh, Daddy," he said in his father's arms as he died. Her father never got over it. "He was broken down for two years," she said. And then it was with him the rest of his life.

There are such things that are with us the rest of our lives. They haunt us day and night. They are the images of failure and despair that we cannot seem to shake. Of course, there are images of success and hope, too, which are also with us day and night. The object is to make sure that the first set of images does not overwhelm the second.

One way to help that happen is with a church. A church reminds us that we are made "in the image of God," which means, among other things, that God wins. God won at the Exodus. God won at Easter. God wins in our lives today when the images of light beat the images of darkness. But how does this latter victory come about?

A young woman had an abortion. It was a tough time for her and her family. Hardly anyone else knew about it. But those who did kept close to her, so much so that her mother said, "This place is oozing with love." It is love that enables us to move from the images of darkness into the images of light.

How could we possibly be loved when we have run over our own child or killed an unborn child? True, such love doesn't make sense, but it is the essence of faith. When the Israelites did not deserve it, then they were loved. "How can I give you up, O Ephraim?" When we least deserved it, we were given Jesus. When we least deserve it, we experience grace.

But aren't there places other than churches where people are loved in spite of what they have done? Of course. Families, places of work, perhaps, service clubs. The difference is that love is the church's job. It is the place where we practice grace. Not that we can do it on our own. Left to our own devices we would not love people in spite of what they had done. The church reminds us that we are not left to our own devices. It is God loving *through* us that enables *us* to love.

The father of the boy who died did not have a church. The young woman has. To be sure, their "failures" may not be comparable in tragedy, but each has his or her images of darkness with which to live. I see her every week. She is one of

13

the most caring young people I know. It would appear that she's passing the love on. The images of light are beating the images of darkness. God is winning.

"Home Sweet Church"

The little girl moved away with her family. Then one weekend she was back visiting a friend. She came to church and afterwards I noticed she had signed the guest book. Beside her name she had written, "Home Sweet Church."

It is remarkable how the experience known as church can be so compelling. In her case her family and friends were here. She came every week. She sang in the children's choir. Of course, that was virtually the same as school, where she went to class every day, sang in the chorus, played with her friends. But would she have written, "Home Sweet School"?

She must have been experiencing something in church she was getting nowhere else. Was it the transcendent? One hopes so. She does not even know what the word means, but the experience is what counts. One experiences love as an infant before naming love as a child. Similarly, one experiences God as a child before naming God as an adult.

It is the church that shows us how to name God. One cannot experience church and fail to discover the word "God" coming increasingly to one's lips. It might even be used in school. It might even be applied to school. If the school is without God, then church hasn't done its job as church.

The job of the church is to help us recognize God in the most astonishing places. If we can say "God" in home, school, office, factory, ball park, then we have experienced "Home Sweet Church."

Plan

You go from the heights to the depths in a single day. A young couple plan their wedding with you. Then you are in the hospital with a college student who has just learned he has a tough disease. Then you are in a home where a child has run away.

The first is easy. It is part of God's plan. But the second and third? How do you say they are part of God's plan? "I know he's trying to teach me something," the college boy said, "but what? What is he trying to tell me? He's got my attention." And he turned away to hide his emotion.

Surprisingly, it was the same with the mother of the teenager who had run away. "He's sure got my attention," she said of God. In both instances they were trying to figure out how their respective dilemmas could be part of God's plan. We don't know; therefore God. It is the opposite of Descartes' celebrated "I think; therefore I am." This is "I don't know; therefore God is." God, it is alleged, is the receptacle into which we hurl our cosmic question marks. God is the crutch we need to make our way through life.

Perhaps. But perhaps not. I have been fascinated by what has happened to these four people. The couple were married. It was a beautiful wedding. They now have a child. At the age of only a few months she developed a health problem which has not yet been fully resolved. People were praying. They still are.

The college student struggled to church the day he got out of the hospital. He wanted to thank everyone for all the love and support. Today he is a businessman, reporting for work at a large corporation in his three-piece suit.

For weeks the mother did not know where her teenager was. She asked us to pray, that some word might come. Finally it did, and she thanked us. Then when the family was reunited, she thanked us again. It was a moving experience each of those Sunday mornings.

What I find fascinating is that these people might have had their respective experiences without the church. They are strong, bright, attractive, well-educated. But each chose to share the experience with other Christians. Maybe their choice was part of God's plan to bring them closer to this people, this parish. Maybe such closeness is all that has yet been revealed of God's plan for them. And maybe that isn't much. But it is something. It is a start.

Surprise

"My wife came after me with a butcher knife. My son decked her. She tried to drown our nine-month-old baby. She kidnapped the two smallest children. I didn't know where they were for eight months. One day they appeared on my doorstep."

My friend is asking for a blessing. He wants to be able to see God in the horror of his life. I am the one he has come to. I pray before he comes and after he leaves. Although I may not feel up to it, I know it is up to me.

It is said that people come to pastors because they are cheap. They never send a bill. Others avoid pastors for the same reason. You get what you pay for, they say. It is also said that people come to pastors because there is no opprobrium should they be discovered. It is one thing to say, "I went to my pastor." It is quite another to say, "I went to my psychiatrist." Few people want it known they have gone to a "shrink."

I have a hunch the real reason people seek out their pastors is a need for God. They want the transcendent to interdict the runaway spiral of their lives. My friend's life is off course. He knows that. And he knows—unconsciously if not consciously—that he needs something as powerful as God to get him back on track.

The question then becomes how best to discover God in the dialogue. The answer is for both of us to be sensitive enough in the moment to be surprised by God, and then to share our surprise. Either of us could make the discovery first. It is the priesthood of all believers. The ambiance is all. I sit with the person. I listen. I offer a question here and there.

In this instance—not in this "case"—the discovery does not come easily. We will meet many times. And we may never discover God. That is the risk we take. It is a risk worth running, however. As Blanche says in Tennessee Williams's play "A Streetcar Named Desire," "Sometimes there is God—so quickly." We are counting on that.

Doubts

"All philosophy begins in wonder," Plato said. That makes a lot of people philosophers. I wonder why the young family has a second retarded child. Why another young mother's child has leukemia. Why a man and a woman are splitting up. Why a sixteen-year-old leaves home to get married. Why a man in his thirties with everything going for him has made only ten thousand dollars in the last two years.

Sometimes the nearest are farthest. The pastor is supposed to be "close to God," but the pastor often feels distant. How do you explain any of the above? "I want answers," a woman said through clenched teeth and tears, as she told me how "devoted" she is to her husband but how she was no longer "in love" with him.

What the pastor has that the philosopher may not is God. With God, our tragedies are perhaps more bearable, if not more comprehensible. The only trouble is, how do you use the word "God" with someone for whom God is a light-year away? I took her hands and held them as she cried.

When she had recovered, she said, "You never have any answers." But *she* has. My job is to hold on while they find her.

God *is* what finds us. It appears that this is the way she has to go to be found. When we are farthest maybe we're nearest. When you're at the opposite end of the earth, the next step brings you closer to home.

Broker

I find myself in a home, an office, a business, factory, hospital, school. Why am I there? There is only one reason—to broker the transcendent. There appear to be other reasons, of course—to be friendly; to sympathize, empathize, care for; to stimulate participation in the life of the church; to express gratitude for such participation when it has occurred. But such reasons are secondary to the primary. The minister calls to broker God.

A broker calls to suggest that you buy or sell. The minister calls to "sell" God. That is to say, when calling on someone, the minister is there to remind that person of the divine dimension. We all live in the dimension of self, which we call psychology. We all live in the dimension of others, which we call sociology. We all live in the dimension of the world around us, which we call ecology. But we do not all live (at least, consciously) in the dimension of God, which we call theology.

The minister goes with one credential—as theologian. The minister is not, strictly speaking, a therapist, except to the extent that the practice of therapy brings an increased awareness of God. Nor is the minister, strictly speaking, a politician, except to the extent that community issues bring an increased awareness of God. Nor is the minister an ecologist, except as the practice of ecology brings people closer to God.

It is at this point that ministers get into trouble. People see them as "practicing psychology" without a degree. They see them on one side of a "political" issue when "their place is in the pulpit." They see them concerned about pollution when "their job is to be concerned about sin."

What people do not see is that these are the minister's attempts to mediate God, to bring the divine dimension to bear on the other three. Admittedly, ministers may not be adept at doing so. But who else is going to do it? Who else is even going to attempt it? Our gravest danger is living life without God. As Dostoevsky said, "Without God we are too strong for one another."

The three dimensions devour each other without the fourth. The water is polluted because it is not seen as God's. People are in trouble because they do not see their problems as opportunities for God. Community issues become community wars because antagonists do not view each other as protagonists who are together trying to work out the will of God.

So when I find myself at a rostrum, a home, or a lake, I do what I can to remind myself, and hopefully the others who are there, that we are on holy ground. More often than not, it is a tough stock to sell. Oil can make ground "holy." But God?

Still Small Voice

"I made $300,000 a year for the last twenty years," he said. "Last year I lost $1.5 million. Now I'm broke. My wife came and took $15,000 worth of furniture. Then she went to my office and took another $4,000. I love God," he said, sobbing. "Help me. Oh, help me."

The minister hears everything. If you can think of it, your pastor has probably heard it. The reason pastors hear so much is that parishioners feel that pastors will not judge. A pastor that does not hear much is perceived as more judging than accepting. This is not to say there is no room for judgment. God judges the wayward Israelites. But first God accepts them.

The pastor listens. Then the pastor tries to elicit God. This is where pastor and psychiatrist differ. The pastor's sole objective is to help the person hear God, even as the person has been heard by the pastor. Note that it is a "person" with the pastor, never a "patient." "Patient" implies inferior; "person" implies equal. The pastor and person are two sinners listening for God.

When people with problems come, the pastor learns from them as well as they from the pastor. Our stories may differ, but there is the same need for acceptance and the same need, in the midst of the whirlwind, to hear the still small voice. The pastor, too, says, "Help me. Oh, help me."

Demon

I often wonder why I am fated to deal with life's imponderables. Most people say that such questions as death and cancer and war and hunger and God are more than one can ever answer. So why bother? Clearly they are right. There *are* no answers when a child dies. But a certain kind of mind is bothered that there are no answers. It is the kind of mind often found in pastors.

I remember being in seminary and having to make a decision. I had just been accepted in a Ph.D. program at Harvard, and the question was whether to stay at the seminary or leave for the university. I stayed, but it was the toughest decision of my life. I remember bouncing from one professor to another to discuss it. Ultimately I decided that, for me, the questions about God were more absorbing than the questions about iambic pentameter.

Absorbing? Compelling would be more accurate. Consuming would be even better. Maybe possessed would be best. We are what possesses us. It goes back to Plato in his "Ion." He wrote of the "demon" that possesses people and will not let them go. It was the Greek way of referring to "god," "fate." We are what we put our energies to. What we live, eat, and breathe, how we sleep and die, is who we are. That is the way it is, for each of us.

Fated? It would seem so. We do not choose our paths. Our "demon" possesses us; we do not possess our "demon." We are possessed by the set of questions that bothers us most. How can I be a good parent? How can I do a good job? How can I be all I was meant to be? It is in the "was meant" that the possession and fating are hinted. "There is a destiny that shapes our ends," Shakespeare said, "rough hew them how we will." We seem destined to be perplexed, and we live out our lives with our separate perplexities. In the pastor's case, it is with life's imponderables.

Night

It was late at night when she called. "Can I come over?" she asked. "Sure," we said. We got dressed and went down and turned the lights on. "Guess what," she said when she arrived, "I don't have it after all," and she named a dread disease. It exploded across our kitchen like a falling star.

When we reached the living room she told us the story. She had been to yet another doctor, they had run some new tests, and they had discovered that no one with her disease could possibly react the way she had. We poured some wine and raised our glasses. I was on the edge of my chair. Jan cried. And she who had come to share her good news sat back on the sofa and beamed.

As she got up to leave, we found ourselves in each other's arms again. We were saying things like "thanks" and "miracle" and "healing" and "love" and "God." God *is* what "heals us of all your diseases," the psalmist wrote. God *is* what "draws us out of the pit" of our despair.

However, the extraordinary thing is that God was as real for her during the original diagnosis as now in this new. That is what says God even more than her sudden good news. People have even used the word "saint" to describe her. Of course, she would have no part of a word like that if she knew. But that is how God works—through saints who, by definition, don't know that they are.

As she walked down our steps and into the night, we called out behind her, "Praise God."

Free Love

Why do the sermons on unconditional love elicit the most response? This morning, person after person came up after the service. One even shot out of the choir to shake my hand and say how much the sermon had meant.

It may be because unconditional love is next-to-impossible. We just don't give it that easily. To tell a thirteen-year-old who is messing up her life that you love her unconditionally is asking a lot.

It may be because unconditional love is most clearly divine. God's number-one attribute in the Bible is "steadfast love." The Bible even says that "God is love." If *we* can't love unconditionally, God can. The Prodigal's father loved his son so prodigiously that he let him go, to almost certain failure. He knew this was the way the young man had to go to be who he was. It was his unconditional love that enabled his son, as the Bible says, to "come to himself."

I remember asking my ten-year-old son if he would like me to read with him. "No," he said; he preferred doing something else at the time. I was hurt, and I showed it. I will love you, I was saying in effect, if you will fit into my agenda. It was the opposite of loving freely.

This is why we need grace. We cannot love freely on our own. Grace is what enables us to love unconditionally. Whenever I love without strings, I have to give the credit to God. It is more than I can do on my own. God is the one who enables me to love freely.

Missed

You came and we talked. It was an interview, you said, for a paper you were doing. You are a "mature" woman in graduate school. As you prepared to leave you said how hard a week it had been. A friend's son, only twenty, had killed himself. Another friend was being slowly killed by cancer.

You seemed to feel it was time to go as you told me these things. Nor did I discourage you. We had been over an hour together. But as you left I felt a need to pray, only neither of us did. I suppose the initiative was mine, but I did not take it. I felt you had come for something more than the interview and that you were not going away with what you had come for. Still, I made no move to pray.

It is now two days later, and I am still feeling we missed something that could have been ours. There was so little we could say to each other about suicide and terminal illness. So you left. And now I am left with feelings that I let you leave too soon. "Let?" That I abandoned you at the point of your deepest need. That we could have said some things to God that we could not have said to each other. That God would have *been* in what we would have said.

I wonder if the notes you took record the same feelings that I have had. I know one thing—I will never skip praying again.

"S'more's"

When she said that her husband called her "a bitch," I could hardly believe what I heard. First, because she said it in a church meeting. Second, because they appear to be happily married. Third, because they are at the heart of the church's life.

What one learns is that "church people" at one level are no different from other people. One may wish that they were. But the fact is that church members are like members of society in general. Often they use the same language. They have the same frustrations. They experience the same wants and needs.

At another level, church people are quite different. They are going for broke. They want it all. It's like our daughter on vacation. She had a teenage friend with her who never goes to church. We were making "S'more's" one night over the fire— marshmallows stuck between squares of chocolate and graham crackers. "That's it," I found myself saying. "That's the reason for church. It gives you something more."

It really comes home on vacation. It's one thing to do your job and go to church because that's how you get your salary or because that's what you do as a family every week. But when you find yourself wanting something more when you're on vacation, and more of the same, then you are experiencing something that has a pretty good hold on you. So off we went, nonchurchgoer and all, to the local Methodist church, where we belted out the hymns and people turned around and looked, wondering who these enthusiasts were.

Without God, something is missing, even in a teenager's life. It's like a "S'more" without the marshmallow. It becomes a "S'less." We laughed about that. She didn't say anything about the service, but I'll bet it got her thinking.

As to the man who speaks that way to his wife, he is in the church because he realizes there is something more to marriage than irritation. He and his wife are in one of our sharing groups with other couples where they have Bible study and prayer and, yes, where they share their bitchiness, upon occasion. In that group he is learning new language. Through the others he is getting something more in his relationship to his wife. It may come as a shock to hear that kind of language in a church meeting, but what is even more surprising is his enthusiasm for something more in his marriage than that. He's roasting his marshmallow, all right.

Confession

"I blew it," you said, as you looked over at your wife. "I blew the one chance I ever had to love." Through your tears you told her you were sorry. You asked her forgiveness. She said she was not at all sure that she could forgive. You said you understood. You said you realized how much pain you had brought her.

It was your confession. You believed it to your very heart. "I can't believe I said those things," you said to me later. You didn't say them, we discovered. God did. And now the way with God will be hard. You no sooner get on it than you are crucified. She won't be back. The really crucial thing will be whether you can continue. There is much going against you. I fear for you.

At the same time I hope. What you said to her in my office was God speaking through you. It was the transcendent lifting you above yourself. There is always hope in that. "I was flabbergasted," you said to me two days later, referring to what you had said. You had every reason to be. God had broken into your life.

Only three weeks before you had lost your job. Now after years of struggle you are losing your wife. But you have found your God. Does it always have to be this way? No. But for you it may. You said it yourself, referring to God's breaking through. "The timing couldn't have been better."

Chapter 2

Jesus in This Parish

Suffering Servant

She is having a difficult time with God right now. Who wouldn't, given her age and all the medical problems she has had? She is young, recently married, and suddenly has a chronic disease. She has been through surgery, been to Mayo's, and now faces several more surgeries as a result of medication. Her difficulty is seeing any evidence of God in all this.

We talk. We pray. We cry. She is angry at what has happened. I am angry at my inability to help her make sense out of nonsense. One way has always been to say it is God's will. But Jesus said, "It is not my Father's will that one of these little ones should perish." Clearly one cannot say God wants her to be ill.

Another way of explaining it is to deny that it is happening, to say that the disease is only a figment of the imagination, that it is not real. But to her it is most certainly real. It is the most real thing in her life, and it threatens to be the most real thing forever.

Another way to make sense out of nonsense is to say she is being punished for her sins. But how can one say that of someone like her? And even if one could, where would be the healing value in such a rationalization as that?

Perhaps that is the source of my frustration. I am trying to make rational what is irrational. It is the inveterate tendency of the mind to explain. Someone has observed that Jesus did not say, "I have explained the world," but "I have overcome the world." In her illness Jesus is "coming over" to her. He is bridging the distance between his death and her life.

Remarkably, she is magnetic. People are drawn to her. When they describe her they use words like "beautiful," "radiant." She may be sick, but she is putting them in touch with health. She is giving them the image of what it means to be Christ-like. She is a suffering servant, as he was, and it is almost as though we have our own Christ in our midst. He is coming over to us because of her.

My job, then, is not to collapse the bridge that she and he are building. It is to resist the temptation to trump up some theological explanation for her illness. As is so often the case, the minister's job is to get out of the way so as not to obscure God. It is also to keep others out of the way so that they do not do the same. When she comes down the hall at church, it is the Lord coming into our lives.

Resurrection Hotel

His wife and daughter were killed by a drunk driver. It put him into a mental hospital for months. When he got out, he went to live with his sister. Her husband had just gotten back from ten years in the penitentiary for murder. Her husband said that her brother embarrassed him in front of his friends by reading the Bible. If he didn't stop, her husband said, he'd blow her brother's brains out.

I called the Jonquil Hotel. Sure, they'd be happy to give him a room. Then I called St. Elizabeth's. They'd be happy to give him meals.

Our church helped a group of Christians buy the hotel a few months ago. They chose the name "Jonquil" because the jonquil, or daffodil, blooming at springtime, is a symbol for resurrection. It is in one of the most run-down areas of the city. The pimps and prostitutes were asked to stop practicing their trade or leave. All but one left. But they have been replaced by gang members. Last week one of them beat two residents senseless and threatened the life of the Good News partner who intervened.

The Good News folks are just that. They have gone into a slum to reclaim it for Christ. First, St. Elizabeth's, the hospitality house, with as many as twenty-eight people a night coming in off the streets, with nowhere else to go. We had a service of worship the first night in the basement among the beds. Then came the hotel. It cost $117,000 and we came up with most of the $32,000 down payment. They've started a health clinic, a church, and a school.

You might think this would not be the place for a recent mental patient. And you may be right. But he will not be there long. He wanted to stay only four days. Those four days he will have the attention he has not had from anyone since his wife and daughter were killed. They will talk to him about Jesus.

"Hello," the man at the desk said as we arrived. "We've been expecting you. Here, let me show you to your room."

Control

I asked the confirmation class to interview their parents on what Jesus Christ meant to them. They came back with paragraphs and tapes. One mother could give only a sentence. Although pressed, she could go no further.

That set me thinking. The purpose of the class is to encourage a child's close, personal relationship with Jesus Christ, but when the child's own mother does not have one, trouble is ahead. It will be difficult for the child if it is already difficult for the parent. Not always, of course, but often.

Possibly what is lacking is an experience of helplessness. If we are not helpless, we don't need Jesus. That is stating it baldly, but that is the way it is. Again, not always, but often. Until we come up against our own limits, we do not need someone else's strength. The child's mother is very much in control of her life— and of her child's. Until she is out of control she will not be controlled.

The movement from active to passive is what this people,

this parish are for. It is among them that we find ourselves moved from controlling our lives to being controlled. That is why you seldom see so-called self-made types in churches. It isn't "virile" to be controlled. It is also why you see church people having what are called "moving experiences." In worship, in small groups, in prayer, in Bible-reading, they find themselves being moved from total control to less control to being controlled. It is why you find church people crying tears of joy—during a service, in silence, in prayer, when visiting a nursing home or jail. They realize they are being moved from running their lives to having their lives run. They say that they are experiencing Christ at work in their lives.

The problem in most churches is that we confirm people at the wrong time. Who wants to experience being out of control at the age of 13 when adolescence is just the time we are learning how to be *in* control? On top of that, when one has a mother teaching one how to be *macho,* one is going to have a tough time indeed giving one's life to Christ. But we plow ahead, hoping his experience in confirmation will be moving enough so that when his crisis comes, the memory will, too.

I got a letter recently from a woman who had been in confirmation years ago. She is now an executive. She is in a crisis. She remembers now what we talked about then and how she gave her life to Jesus.

Hors d'Oeuvres

It was a spectacular affair. One-sixth of the church was there. The old, the young, even spouses and friends who were not members. It was one of our all-church get-togethers, which we have every three months or so. At the moment, we were eating hors d'oeuvres in one home, and then we would split up to go to other homes for dinner.

I was thinking how much this people, this parish mean to each other. Here we were, just a group of people, gathered from everywhere, some not even knowing each other until now, in the suburb of a metropolis, on a Friday night in May, having a good time. As I went from cluster to cluster, it occurred to me that none of us would know each other unless we were, in some sense, known.

It is this being known that is a hallmark of churches. There are plenty of organizations one can belong to without being known as a consequence of membership. Not so the church. One joins a church in part because one is known or wants to become known. Jesus not only went about doing good, he went about revealing people to themselves. He wanted them to know who they were so they could be what they might become.

Each of the people that night was revealing part of him- or herself to the others—not much at a social event like this, but some. And they were doing so because they had been, or were being, revealed to themselves. When one has a relationship to Jesus, one is involved not only in self-acceptance but self-discovery. "He told me all that I ever did," exclaimed the woman at the well. "I came that they may have life," he said, "and have it abundantly." The Prodigal Son was being called to abundance. The Good Samaritan was living a full life.

The great psychologist William James once observed that we function at only ten percent of capacity. A relationship with Jesus can open up the remaining ninety percent. So can a relationship to LSD, it is argued. Or to yoga. Or Buddha. Or to the Puritan work ethic. Or art. Or communism, or democracy. What is different about Jesus? It is a relationship with a person. Buddha was a person. But he didn't allow himself to be killed, in Bonhoeffer's phrase, in love to the uttermost. There is something in Jesus' total self-giving that is totally self-revealing, that opens up the remaining ninety percent of who we are.

How, then, does one show that he or she is related to Jesus? Through revealing oneself to other people, as at a church party, however modest such self-revelations may be. And where is the motivation for such self-revelation? From the experience one has already had, or is in the process of having, with Jesus. As Jesus is revealed to us, we are moved to reveal ourselves to others. As we are moved to reveal ourselves to others, Jesus is revealed to us. The two types of revelation reinforce each other. Each motivates the other.

Where does it all start? Most likely, but not necessarily, with someone else who, as Jesus, gave him- or herself in love to the uttermost for us.

Evangelism

We put her into her grave, and we have not seen him since. Of course, we had not seen him before either. But now that he needs us more than ever, you'd think he would be close to this people, this parish. He gave some money in her memory. He wrote a nice note. And there has been no sign of him since.

How can such a person not need us? It is a mystery to those in a church. Is it our own need to be needed? If so, then he should avoid us. Or is it that we have something we want to share, some new life that makes sense even of death? If so, then we should not avoid him.

But we are adept at avoiding. He has made his choice. He is a grown man. He knows what he needs. He knows where we are. If he needs us, he will call. Until then, it is not our place to call him. But is that line of thinking correct? If so, then Christianity would never have made it out of Nazareth. Jesus left home and called on twelve people, none of whom had come to him, and with those twelve, as the Book of Acts says, he "turned the world upside down."

Our reluctance is largely cultural. We have been acculturated not to call on people who do not ask us. In business it is different. We make cold calls to sell. But that is business. One will do anything to earn a living. But to share one's new life, to share Jesus, that is another matter. When we are not driven by economic necessity, we pull back.

What can take the place of economic necessity? Is there such a thing as religious necessity? I was in a hardware store, and the owner was wearing a cross. I remarked on it, and we fell into conversation. He goes to Bible study every Sunday at ten, then church at eleven, and during the week he assists with the youth group. His eyes were aglow as he told me. He couldn't wait to introduce me to his wife and clerk who were, as he said, also Christians. Two days later I was back at his store to introduce him to my wife.

Something is missing when we do not share the new life we have found—more accurately, that has found us. I am naïve enough to think that something—someone—is missing from the bereaved husband's life. Now that his wife is gone, it is our job to show him what's missing. If he pulls back, that is his prerogative. But "necessity is laid upon me," Paul said, to go.

Grace

"Just another ho-hum Sunday," he said, as we looked up from prayer around 1:00. He says it nearly every Sunday now. He's joking, of course, but others are picking it up. It is becoming a byword, as people dry their eyes after prayer and go down the hall hugging each other and inviting strangers for lunch.

There was a time when he would not have said it. He wasn't even in church. Then it happened. I have no idea how. But the Damascus Road came for him as it did for Paul. He has been irrepressible since. He can't get enough of Sunday, or retreats, or reading the Bible, or being with people who hurt, as well as with those who laugh.

Maybe I do have an idea. His son left home. He was the last child to go. There had been problems. His business was dreary. Golf had palled. Drink had taken its toll. Nothing dramatic. "What a gift God gave me," he said to me once. "He got hold of me before I stumbled and fell."

You can never explain these things. They happen and they do not happen. "You turn me off," he told me one of his friends said to him, "when you talk about all these religious things." His friend doesn't need them. The right constellation of events has not yet occurred for his friend. Perhaps it never will.

On the other hand, my friend's turnabout makes it easier to believe in grace. He had nothing to do with his new life. It was beyond his control. He did not will it. He did not plan it. He was just living out his life. Then it happened. The timing was right. Grace is what happens to us. Faith is our response to what happens. Works are what then happen through us.

Why did the one man respond and the other not? We'll never know. "At the right time, Christ died" for us, Paul said. That is all we will ever know.

Timing

He said he had committed his life to Jesus, and he wanted to tell me about it. I urged him to tell others, too. He said he would not have made the commitment if "the right set of circumstances" had not occurred in his life. I said I believed it.

Timing is everything in the Christian life. Such commitments cannot be made until a person is ready. "The readiness is all," Shakespeare wrote. Jesus comes, one reads in Ephesians, "in the fulness of time." And until that time comes, one cannot come to Jesus.

It is different for everyone. Some people give their lives to Jesus at an early age. Others on their deathbeds. Others in between. One cannot predict. One cannot legislate. "The wind blows where it wills," Jesus said to Nicodemus, whose time had not yet come.

Later Nicodemus was to stand up for Jesus in the Sanhedrin, the only man to do so. "Does our law judge a man," he asked, "without first giving him a hearing?" Still later, it was Nicodemus who helped Joseph of Arimathea bring the body of Jesus down, at great risk to himself. His commitment had come long after his first encounter with Christ.

The mystery of timing renders confirmation suspect; also suspect are datable conversion experiences as a condition of church membership. An entire class of thirteen-year-olds cannot be expected to have committed their lives to Jesus. Sometimes only one or two have; sometimes none; rarely all. The timing is individual. As my friend said, there has to be the "right set of circumstances."

In the letter to the Ephesians it is called God's "plan." God has the right timing in mind. We do not know what that plan is, but when the final grain of sand has been placed on the scales and they tip, then we know. When Nicodemus came to Jesus that first time, already the scales had begun to tip, although he did not know it. But by the time he was risking ostracism for bringing the body of Jesus down, then he knew.

There is a sense, then, in which all one can do is watch and wait. True, Nicodemus came to Jesus, but he came in response to Jesus' being there. The action is always responsive. The initiative is God's, not ours. We cannot claim anything in coming to Christ. "No one can come to me," Jesus said, "unless the Father who sent me draws him." It is the events of our lives that, one at a time, are drawing us to Jesus. Then, at the right time, the commitment is made. The final grain of sand has been placed. One finds oneself risking all for him.

Periphery

I go from place to place downtown. Someone works here, someone there. I am making my rounds. People are not in, can't see me, have only a few minutes. But my being there is a simple reminder of this people, this parish in a parishioner's week. It is modest evidence for Christ in a person's day.

Occasionally it doesn't work, at least not the way I would hope. Some of the calls are on people who are peripheral to the life of the church. What my call does is seal their decision to leave. I can see myself now in the places where we talked, I in my chair, they in theirs. It was just an attempt to bridge a social gap, nothing more; to express friendship, Christ. Within a few weeks or months they are gone. Not always, of course, but occasionally.

As I think about it, what I am doing in such instances is calling too late. Attendance has slipped. I have picked up inklings from others. But to call on such people has been low in priority. After all, one has all one can do to keep up with those who are central, let alone peripheral. Surely the doctor does not call on those who have dropped him or her as a doctor.

Jesus told the story of the lost sheep—how the shepherd got them all in the fold except one, and how he promptly searched until he found it. So, one searches and does one's best. But Jesus also told his disciples to shake the dust off their feet and go on to the next town if they were not accepted. There is only so much searching one can do.

Moving from the periphery to the center is clearly a two-way street. The pastor or deacon or other church member moves from the center to the periphery. But then the peripheral one must also move toward the center. And the key to that is apparently his or her sensing the slide toward the periphery before it is too late and the motivation has gone.

But if even that has not worked, what then? One people, one parish should not be so smug as to think that they have the only way to experience Christ. Peripheral parishioners should be encouraged to seek another church where they can experience Christ better. Next time I am in a chair opposite such a person, I will encourage him or her to do so, if there is no desire to return to our church. Such candor can only be spiritually helpful to all concerned.

Distance

"You couldn't get me here if you had a $100 check waiting for me every week." I admire the honesty but not the diligence. "There is no way," he went on to explain, "that I can treat Sunday any other way than as just another part of the weekend. The ritual is meaningless. And the hymns are too high."

In view of the fact that he has only been to church twice in the last year, I was not impressed. I took him on. We went back and forth. These kinds of comments are always the tip of the iceberg. What was underneath soon became apparent. "I believe that Jesus was a prophet but not the Son of God."

Many people in churches have never had a close, personal relationship with Jesus Christ. It's the heart of the matter for Christians, no matter what their tradition. They have to be close to Christ. If they're not, Sunday morning, let alone anything more, is out of the question.

We got into "anything more," too. "What's more," he said, "I want distance in my relationships. I don't want to be close. I want to choose the people I want to be close to and, frankly, I don't want to be close to some of the people in this church. I don't even know them."

It's the old story. How can we be close to Christ, whom we have not seen, if we do not want to be close to his people, whom we have seen? The church is a laboratory for this kind of closeness. In my experience, people who have trouble "accepting Christ" are often those who have trouble accepting others. And people who have trouble accepting others are often, in my experience, people who have trouble accepting themselves. One way to improve self-acceptance is to see yourself being accepted by others.

I was in a Christian group last night. We are in a covenant relationship, trying to learn more about prayer and meditation. One person said she thinks of God as mother. Another said he didn't think of God at all—no image. Another said prayer isn't worth anything unless it results in action. We were close. We could say anything because we accepted each other. That helped each of us in terms of our own self-acceptance. And our own self-acceptance, in the ambiance of our coming together, made it easier to accept Christ.

I'd give anything for this businessman friend of mine to be in such a group. But in our head-to-head encounter, it was no sale. Now I have to live with his failure to "buy." First, I have to live with the fact that I couldn't "sell." Second, I have to live with trying to figure out how to try again. Third, I have to live with my inertia about doing anything more. After all, businessmen don't spend much time trying to win back disaffected customers. They have their hands full as it is.

It troubles me, and I've been thinking about it this week. The ball is now in his court. We left it that, since I had taken this initiative, he would call me after we had each thought about some of the things the other had said. That was six years ago.

Transparence

He tells me how I have changed. "Wow!" he says. He likes the change, and I need him to verify it to me. I have been feeling it myself, and now he is confirming it. He sees a "deepening," as he puts it. When I ask him to explain, he says that he is better able to see Jesus through me now than before.

We need each other in order to "see" Jesus. That is how he becomes visible. We see Jesus in the other. Our job in this parish is to be transparent to Jesus. So often we are opaque, occasionally translucent, rarely transparent. It is these moments of transparency on which the beloved community thrives.

One way to tell they are happening is to have them affirmed. Otherwise the transparency is not always apparent. I felt myself changing, but it was only a hunch. I needed my friend to tell me he saw it. "If anyone is in Christ," Paul wrote, he or she is "a new creation." We need this people, this parish to affirm our newness.

One cannot always see it oneself. That is why Christianity is not a religion that can be done in isolation. We need others to say what they see. But it takes courage to say what my friend said. Most of us are timid. We are embarrassed to go to another and tell him or her we can see Jesus better now.

The priesthood of all believers, as it has been known since Luther's time, has many dimensions. The basic one is that each is a priest to all. That is, we are part of a people, a parish in order to reveal Christ to those in the parish. Our job is not only to see Christ in others but to show Christ ourselves. And not only to those in the parish but beyond.

It is hard to identify what my friend saw. One hesitates to say how one is transparent to Christ. But something has happened over the last several months that has been good. It has deepened a number of us. I passed a church member in a hospital parking lot. We got to talking and went in to have lunch together. Out of that came the idea of a Saturday morning men's group, and we have been meeting every week since over donuts and coffee from 8:00 to 9:00.

When ten to twenty convene for the sole purpose of being transparent to Jesus, using Scripture, sharing, and praying, something is likely to happen; change may well occur. "A deepening," my friend said. "A new visibility," he explained when pressed. And it is in him and the others, too.

Self-Acceptance

"Once a week for thirty years I've been over the edge on alcohol. I've been immature for so long. But Tuesday the fourteenth I said, 'Jesus, I will never drink again.' One of the few things I am proud of in my life is that my word is my bond. I always worried about killing someone when I was drunk. I was so guilt-ridden I felt I was responsible for everything except starting World War II. I got a letter from my daughter. 'You may think you're a failure, Dad,' she said, 'but you're not as a father.' I feel a four-hundred-pound load of guilt lifted."

The view we have of ourselves determines how we behave. If we like ourselves we act one way; if we do not, we act another. One way to right acting is right thinking. And one way to think right is to be accepted by a group of people who take us as we are. If my friend had had such a group all along, things might have been different. As it was, he came to this people, this parish somewhat later in life, but not too late. It has been almost three years now since he had a drink. Not that drinking was the problem, but, as he himself acknowledged, it was a powerful symptom.

Where do this people, this parish get their ability to accept us in spite of ourselves? From their experience of being accepted in spite of themselves. It's what the Bible calls grace, and for Christians it comes from being close to Christ, who accepted people even when they despised him. But more than that, his acceptance of people made them feel good about themselves. The woman at the well who had had five husbands must have felt as badly about herself as my friend did about himself. Jesus' acceptance of her enabled her to accept herself and so see herself for who she was. She ran back to the city to tell everyone in sight.

It was no accident that my friend was telling me about what had happened to him. Nor was it an accident that he described it in terms that included Jesus. In the Christian context, when one feels forgiven, when one feels a 400-pound load of guilt lifted, one finds oneself saying the name, "Jesus." It is people who say the name "Jesus" to each other who provide a right atmosphere for others to think well of themselves. It is no accident that my friend's behavior changed so radically when he and his wife were visiting in the home of some Christian friends. These friends spoke of how their own view of themselves had recently changed, and how they had begun to find themselves using the name, "Jesus." It was that weekend he said, "Jesus, I will never drink again."

Acceptance

"I think I'd die without this church," he said. "I couldn't do it on my own." He is highly successful. He has a fine family. And he makes an admission like this.

What does the church have that prompts such enthusiasm? He listed the choir, Bible study, Sunday mornings, the men's group on Saturdays. He gets these nowhere else. But there has to be more. These alone are not sufficient to produce such extravagance.

It is this people, this parish. They are what sustain him. He relates to them differently from the way he relates to the people at work. There he is what he does. Here he does what he is. There is a difference. There he is judged on his performance. Here he is not judged.

This is not to say that performance-judgments are not valid. Clearly they are. They make the economy work. But they are perhaps less valid in church. Church is where we accept each other for who we are rather than judge each other for what we do.

It is this alternating rhythm in his life to which my friend responds. At church, being complements doing. He feels he is accepted for the person he is, not for the work he does. He knows that he can never "work" enough. He can never measure up. He can never meet the performance standards. He will always fall short. The company could always be better run.

At church, he is accepted in spite of his shortcomings. It is the difference between Paul the Pharisee and Paul the Christian. "The good that I would," Paul discovered, "I do not; the evil that I would not, that I do." He was always falling short. His discovery was that his work wouldn't work. He had to be saved from thinking it would. It was then that he met his Savior.

When my friend met Jesus, it made all the difference. At last the driven executive was loved for who he was as well as paid for what he did. He discovered Jesus through the people in his

42

church. Their unconditional acceptance of him enabled him to accept himself unconditionally. At last he knew what Jesus meant when he said, "Love your neighbor as yourself." He loved himself, for perhaps the first time in his life.

Why does the church do it? Why does it accept people as they are? Because the people in the church feel they have been accepted as they are. That is what meeting Christ means. He gives people the ability to accept themselves in spite of all their failures to measure up. He gave that ability to Matthew, the tax collector. He gave it to Peter, the part-owner of a fishing business, who could never catch enough fish. He gave it to the woman at the well. He thought he had given it to Judas, the revolutionary.

Faith is the feeling people have of being loved in spite of themselves, in spite of all their attempts to perform superbly. My talented friend came to realize that he could never be superb enough. It was then, as with Paul, that Christ could enter his life. And he did it through others who had already come to the realization that they, too, could never be superb enough yet were somehow loved, regardless.

Chapter 3

The Holy Spirit
in This Parish

New Church

"We've been gone three years," she said, "and we can't find a church like this." I'm not sure she should try. It is a frequent lament. People grow fond of their churches. It is hard to leave. But trying to duplicate them elsewhere is certain to fail.

Each church is unique. It has its history, people, traditions. It is open to the Holy Spirit in its own way. What works with one people, one parish may not work with another. Such attempts at duplication are grafting a strange flesh, and they rarely take.

What is needed when church members move is what Coleridge called "that willing suspension of disbelief which alone constitutes poetic faith." We need the religious faith that different is not always worse. Indeed, it could even be better. At the very least, it could be a new way of experiencing the Spirit.

Ministers have the same problem moving to new churches. Often they expect people to react the way people did in the old. It is a setup for failure. When I came here eight years ago, I tried to put all former "successes" out of my mind. A new people, a new parish had to be understood in a new way. I keep having to suspend disbelief that the Holy Spirit could come in such new ways, even ways that may not have worked before.

Having said that, there are, naturally, common denominators that one looks for in a new church. One is warmth. It is hard to incubate fire in ice. And it was fire that was the first manifestation of the Holy Spirit in the church. "My heart was strangely warmed," John Wesley wrote. It was his description of the Holy Spirit taking over his life. If you are not warmly welcomed in a church, it may be right to move on. The first time I met the committee from this church, the meeting ended with people embracing. I knew immediately this was a place I would like to be.

46

Another common denominator is openness. How open is the church to the exercise of your gift? "To each is given a manifestation of the Spirit," Paul wrote, "for the common good." What is it you love to do that, when you do it, makes you lose all track of time? That is your gift, and if you cannot share it with your church, then you had best move on. Only those churches that are hospitable to a variety of gifts and that actually encourage the use of individuals' gifts are churches worthy of being identified as "Christian."

With a willing suspension of disbelief on the trail of warmth and openness, one is likely to find a new church that fits. As a visitor said to one of our people the other day after church: "We've visited every church in the area for the last year-and-a-half. Today we found what we were looking for." It can happen, and, more often than not, it does.

Interruption

"I am not unwilling to work. I'm honored to be asked. But I have a timing problem." It is a response that one sometimes hears when church members are asked to become church officers.

When is the Holy Spirit's timing ever "right?" "This night your soul is required of you," Jesus said in one of the Gospel parables. When someone was addressed by Jesus with the words "Follow me," he objected: "First let me bury my father." Jesus had a lot of trouble with people who, when the call came, declined to answer affirmatively.

I think of the people who accept. It is almost always immediate or within a day or so. Such people are invariably as busy as those who decline.

Peter had a timing problem. He was busy trying to make a living at the fishing business. Moses had a timing problem. It wasn't the right time to go to the very place where he was wanted for murder. But he went.

If you look at the promptings of the Spirit in the Bible, you don't find many instances where there was not a "timing problem." If they all had waited around until the timing was right, there would have been very few prophets and disciples. It may even be that a call is a call by the very nature of the timing problem. If it interrupts your plans, that just may prove it is a call. As Dietrich Bonhoeffer once said, "We must allow ourselves to be interrupted by God."

To be sure, there are instances where someone is sufficiently involved elsewhere that it would be manifestly inappropriate to become as involved in the church. But such instances, in my experience, are rare. More often, it seems, the "timing problem" is a rationalization, not a reason.

Yet, we never push. If a person cannot see that the inconvenience might be proving the call, we back off. We simply go on to someone else. That is why it sometimes takes church nominating committees a long time to finish their work. But I am not at all sure we are doing it right. Can you imagine God backing off from the call to a busy young woman to give birth to Jesus?

Planning

I am on the edge of my chair these days. I don't know what it is. Maybe it is just that the new church year is beginning. Summer is over and people are coming back. But I think it is more than that. A wind is blowing. Our church is moving dangerously close to the Spirit.

I say "dangerously" because, with the Spirit, you never know what's going to happen. You cannot predict. You cannot plan. You cannot control. "The wind blows where it wills" is what

Jesus said. And since you cannot control the wind, you worry. It brings me to the edge of my chair, maybe as much to be ready for what's going to happen as any other reason.

Only a few years ago I wrote a book on church planning. I haven't looked at it here. I am beyond that. Not that "beyond" means better. Only different. The Spirit is working differently in my life. There is fresh evidence.

Take this lack of desire to plan. It's because I have the feeling that an unplanned church may be as spiritual as a planned one. All the first Christians did after the Crucifixion was sit around in that upper room and pray. That's all we're doing. The evidence that puts me on the edge of my chair is all these people in this church praying. And what is prayer but asking to be led rather than to lead, asking to be controlled rather than to control, to be planned rather than to plan?

Now, of course, this approach is not the easiest in the world to sell to people who make their living planning. People who manage offices and homes and labor unions and political parties are fanatics on the subject of planning. And they are, of course, right, up to a point. But now it is time to make a different point. The first Christians did not draw up a "management plan" for how they were going to convert the world. They *were* planned *by* the Spirit and then went out and "turned the world upside down."

Case in point. A man and I got together yesterday to pray with each other and share where we were in the spiritual life. Two hours later a weekly "Men's Relational Bible Study" had been planned. That is, it had planned itself. It sprang organically from the spiritual process of prayer and sharing rather than springing from the planning process.

We cast about for who could lead the Bible study. We fixed on a church member who is gifted in this way. But he isn't even in the state at the moment. "We don't need him," my friend said. "I'll do it." He's committed because we planned from within rather than from without. The plan came out of the prayer rather than the prayer coming out of the plan. That's why I'm on the edge of my chair these days.

Something There

"When it takes you an hour to get out of church, you know something's there." That's as far as she could go. But it was pretty far. She was saying it to the church board, trying to explain why she was joining the church.

It happens every time we take in a new group. They try to put their reasons into words, and it never quite clicks. Of course, if it could click maybe something would be lost. You can say a lot about the Holy Spirit and many have. But one thing all would agree on is that the experience of the Spirit is indescribable.

Her inarticulateness about her spiritual life was contagious. Heads nodded and there were murmurs of assent. People were responding to the fact that "something's there." Something was there for them, too, or they would not have joined some time ago or be joining now.

If we could catch what cannot be caught and say what cannot be said, it would not be religion. Religion connotes more than it denotes, and when we try to be concrete about the abstract we get only so far. And that is all right. It lets God be God. Still, we make our attempts, and that is all right, too. After all, God made an attempt, first in a people, then in a person to say, "I'm here." "Something's there" is the response of the Spirit to "I'm here."

Senior "Punk" Highs

Bob—

We spent a lot of time trying to clean your office but every time we moved it just got worse—we'll do it again if you want us to!

50

Love,
The Senior "Punk" Highs

P.S. Your office is cleaner than its ever been except its a little bit glittery.

The note was on my desk after Wednesday night "Bob Talk." Twenty or so senior highs gather in my office during Youth Club, and we talk about whatever comes into our heads, mostly my head since they want me to be in charge of the agenda. On this particular night they had festooned themselves in "Punk" glitter, and after our time together was over, the evidence of their presence was everywhere. Several stayed behind to clean up while I went on to a board meeting.

I love them. It's as simple as that. We have the grandest times. Our meetings each week are bedlam, but something seems to happen. Like the time we all prayed for one of the group who was going to have an operation. Or the time we listened to another tell of a home conflict that seemed irreconcilable. It grew quiet. No one will forget those moments, or the happy chaos either.

Two of my glittering friends are at the moment in the jungles of Panama. A third is in Paraguay. One wrote me that a deadly snake had just been killed in front of his hut. Another that the food was so bad and the climate so hot and the accommodations so miserable that some of the group might not make it. The group is called Amigos ("Friends") and is known nationwide through high school Spanish classes. They dig latrines and teach people how to clean their teeth and other matters of basic hygiene.

What impresses me is not only that they are there but that they are there, in part, because of The Senior "Punk" Highs. They are getting something here they don't get anywhere else. Yes, it's a social life that cuts across the usual cliques in high schools. Yes, it's a lot of fun, as they do everything from amusement parks to lock-ins. Yes, they have fine, young professional leadership.

But none of that quite says it. None of that quite describes what you can get in a church youth group that you don't get anywhere else. Maybe it's the Holy Spirit. I know, that sounds like a copout. It sounds like the substitute of a hackneyed phrase for a clear description. But maybe the old phrases of the Bible are old precisely because they work, precisely because we *can't* be more precise.

The kids would be "blown away" if you told them they were there because of the Holy Spirit. There'd be that happy chaos for a moment. But then it might get strangely quiet. It just might be one of those moments they wouldn't forget. The Holy Spirit is why one of the boys in Panama could write: "I miss the church and the youth group a lot." And then he signed his letter, "Love."

Fire

"I'm scared," she said through her tears. "I'm desolate. When is it going to end? For the first time I feel hopeless. Only a miracle can save me now." But then as we bowed our heads in her hospital room she prayed, "Thank you for Bob, for his love, for the church and their love."

I was astounded. That one in her condition could be thinking of others at such a time was inspiring. The word "inspire" comes from the root for "spirit within." Clearly, she was possessed by the Spirit, because what she said could not have been said on her own.

The church are the people who share the Spirit with each other, who reveal the Spirit *in* each other. Something had happened because someone had come from the church. She was so much a part of this people, this parish that when one of them came to be with her, the Holy Spirit came, too. When you are afraid of dying, yet can pray for others rather than for yourself, it seems clear that it is something more than you that is doing the praying.

"The Spirit," Paul wrote, "intercedes for us with sighs too deep for words." Jesus, dying on the cross, pleads for those killing him. Stephen does the same. It was so inspiring that Paul was converted. The one holding the jackets of the mob while they dropped rocks on Stephen's head was so astounded by what he heard that the Spirit took possession of him.

But note what happened. The Spirit came through another. It is not enough in the Christian tradition to sit under a tree and expect to be touched by the Spirit. More likely than not the Spirit will come when one is touched by someone who has already been touched. Church members are flint to each other's steel, and the resultant fire, to use the word associated with Pentecost, can warm them all. They were all together when Pentecost happened.

She has touched virtually every life in the parish. Everyone knows of her fear, her desolation, her hopelessness. But everyone also knows how much the Holy Spirit is speaking through her to others' fear, desolation, hopelessness. Her ability to inspire has carried to every corner of the church. But she would be the last to believe it and would never admit it.

Such modesty is a mark of the Spirit. It is characteristic of inspiring people that they take no credit for inspiring anyone. It is proof that the inspiring is being done through them, by the Spirit, rather than by them. I left the hospital taking the steps two at a time.

Joy

"They told us no God. They told us when we die we are dust. They made the churches into houses for soldiers. They said religion thought up to fool us."

He was only seventeen when they left Vietnam. They were attacked three times by pirates. A girl jumped overboard. They never saw her again. They languished over a year in an Indonesian camp.

Now he was in my office. His three friends had just been killed in an accident. They were on their way to visit other refugees. Two were killed instantly; the third lingered three days. They had asked him to go with them, but he had worked late that night and was tired.

He was asking me how to join the church. I gave him the material to read. We talked about God and Jesus. I gave him a Bible. We prayed. He said he couldn't sleep nights. We prayed again and imagined Jesus with him then. He smiled as he left.

On the Sunday of his joining he came early to church. He said he wanted to confess. We bowed our heads in my office. When it came time for him to come forward, I asked those whose lives had touched his to come forward with him. They came, whole families at a time. And when I asked him to kneel, they reached out and touched him. When he got up, there were tears in his eyes. And when he left church that Sunday, on his way to the parking lot, he threw up his hands in joy.

It seems as though we need help to come to Christ. Something outside us brings us. God is active in the events of our lives. They are what draw us to Christ. They can be positive or negative. In his case it was tragedy that brought him. In other cases it is the good things that happen. At the time of marriage, for instance, we are prompted to say, "God is someone I thank for someone I love." For many, it is the first theological statement of their adult lives.

Either way, positive or negative, it is the events of our lives that bring us. We do not come to Christ; we are brought. "No one can say 'Jesus is Lord,' " Paul observed, "except by the Holy Spirit." The Spirit is the one who moves through the events of our lives to show us that Jesus is in them. He is an omnipotent Person, not just an impersonal force.

When people marry, they leave the church with hands thrown up in joy. Wherever joy is, God is. And when a person leaves church after an unspeakable tragedy and throws up his hands in joy, that is God, too. "You rejoice," Peter wrote his friends who were, as he was, under constant threat of execution, "with unutterable and exalted joy."

Synthesis

It was announced in church that he would have his surgery that week. We prayed for him. Afterwards we prayed again. There must have been thirty people in my office. We all reached forward to him. Those in the back had their hands on those who held him.

Many prayed aloud. There were those who could pray directly for healing and those who could not. It did not matter. What mattered was the powerful release of the Holy Spirit, which everyone felt. And he especially. He sat there when the last "Amen" had been said, and there was a quiet smile on his face.

It is generally true that it is those who have not experienced the power of the Holy Spirit who need to keep trying to define it further. It is as though the definition could bring the experience. But after Jesus' death, the disciples and their friends did not sit around in the Upper Room attempting to describe what had happened to them. The Bible says they prayed. It is most significant that we experienced the Holy Spirit when we, too, prayed.

Why this need for constant analysis? Some of the most brilliant analyzers I know were in that room. For the moment, in the moment, they were able to put their analytical minds on hold and bring their synthesizing minds on line. And all because they were confronted with a problem that defied analysis but yearned for synthesis.

The power of the Holy Spirit brings things together. "Synthesis" comes from the Greek for "put together." When we pray, we are trying, as we say, to "put it all together." We are hoping for a moment of fusion when the disparate strands of our lives will cohere. It is such moments that we call God. And it is the ability to release them that we call God's power, or the Holy Spirit.

Imprecise? Perhaps. But for those who have experienced it, not at all.

Unsung Heroes

I heard a noise at the other end of the building, and there he was, under the balcony, late at night. He looks after the church for us and was making his rounds. But late at night?

There are probably one or two people like this in almost every church. We have two who help out in the office every week. There appears to be nothing remarkable in that. Most churches have such people. What is remarkable is their average tenure—fourteen years.

Every church has its unsung heroes. Year in and year out they are there. Through all the challenges of church life, through all the pastors, choir directors, secretaries, and custodians, they are there. Through all the vicissitudes of their own lives, getting the kids off to school, caring for dying parents, preparing for dinner parties and Scout weekends, they are there.

It is this staying power which is as much a gift of the Spirit as any of the more familiar Christian virtues, such as faith, hope, and love. "Endurance," Paul calls it, and it is one of the great words of the Bible. Had the early Christians not had it in such rich abundance, none of us would likely be Christians now.

There is another gift of the Spirit which seems to fit such people. It is humility. When I say they are unsung heroes, it is just that. Most of the people in the church do not even know they do these things. And when they do know, hardly anyone compliments them. Maybe that's because their years of service seem to be as much a part of the church as the cornerstone, and compliments appear to be superfluous. At any rate, they do not do their jobs to be complimented. The mere doing of them is thanks enough. More to the point, if they can be humble servants of Christ, that is all they ask.

I thanked my friend for what he was doing under the balcony. He was still at the church when I left.

Whistler

We have a church secretary who whistles. It is most unusual. Not that people don't like their work. Most whom I know do. But whistlers are few and far between, at least in my experience.

I have even caught her singing. But "caught" is not right. She doesn't mind who "catches" her. Her exuberance is perennial. It is also contagious. Some even go away humming.

"Who is that who just answered the phone?" I have been asked. It is our whistler. Sales people and repair people love her. She treats them as equals. Church people love her. She treats them as equals, too. Everyone gets a joke, an offer of coffee, often a hug.

She dances. Yes, I have "caught" her doing a jig in the middle of the hall. And for what reason? No reason. She doesn't need "reasons." It was a beautiful day? Perhaps. It was a terrible day. Why not? She had more work than she could possibly get done that day? Of course, time for a jig.

Paul said that the fruit of the Spirit includes love, joy, and peace. We remember the love and peace but sometimes forget the joy. Clearly, Jesus was full of the "joy of the Lord." I have a picture of him in my office with his head thrown back. He is obviously relishing a joke.

Without a joyful outlook, Paul wouldn't have been Paul. It is a matter of historical record that the first Christians sang on their way to their executions. Macabre? Hardly. They knew the joy of the Lord.

Imagine my surprise, then, when my whistler announced she was leaving. She had accepted a call to mission work. She would give her life to the poor wherever her church needed her. Needless to say, I was devastated.

But could I not be a whistler, too? Could I not dance with delight at this greater call to service? Could I not hum her on her way? It was hard, but eventually, after she gave me a severe talking to, I was able. As I say, whistlers are contagious. They are the Holy Spirit at play.

Where Did You Go?

As the children came up for the children's sermon, you came all the way that Sunday and sat beside me and put your head on my shoulder. You were in the fifth grade then. Three years later you were in the confirmation class, and when we met each other in the hall those afternoons we would embrace. Last month I saw you at the church's ice cream social on the Fourth of July. I was singing the patriotic songs with the others on the steps. You waved at me vigorously from the crowd.

Where did you go between confirmation and last month? It's been three years again, and the group has wondered where you've been. Once I passed you on the street. I rolled my window down. We talked until a car came up behind.

We read about the rich young ruler in the confirmation class and how Jesus issued him the challenge to sell what he had and give to the poor and how he turned away sorrowing and left Jesus. But that is not the situation for you. You may not be meeting the challenge of youth group or church, but I know you are meeting others. You are popular. You are in the musicals at school. You get good grades. Word comes back to me how well things are going for you.

Why have you wandered so far from us? Where is the Holy Spirit taking you?

"Do you know how much I miss you?" I ask through the open car window.

"I miss you, too," you say.

We squeeze each other's hand. I drive on to Youth Club. You walk up the driveway to your home.

Chapter 4

The Bible in This Parish

Mystery

She went away saying it was "the most exciting hour of the week." She was referring to the Sunday morning Bible study before church. Either she had had a drab week or she was saying something worth attention. In view of the fact that her life is full and her interests many, it is probably the latter.

There is something in the Book that compels attention. Her life may be full, but it could always be fuller. The Bible brings her a measure of fullness she gets nowhere else. Why? It is hard to say. Maybe it doesn't have to be explained, only accepted. The Bible fulfills us as nothing else.

Is it the language? In part. Is it the themes? Yes. The fact that it is inspired? Yes. That one "meets God" there? Certainly. But one can meet God anywhere. Much art is "inspired." One hears a lofty theme at the end of Beethoven's Ninth, and the language of Shakespeare is often as arresting as that of the Bible.

Maybe the Bible is one of the few places all these happen together. Perhaps it has a fullness of its own. Maybe that is why she is excited. Then, too, she is discussing it with ten or twenty others. We are Augustine's "church within the church."

But there has to be more. None of these explanations alone is satisfactory. Nor do all of them together explain how the Bible could provide the most exciting hour of someone's week. Maybe she is given to hyperbole. But she isn't. Maybe it was an access of enthusiasm after one particularly good session. But it wasn't. She has said it on several occasions. Maybe she is high-strung, given to flights of the imagination. But she isn't. Maybe she has psychological problems. But she hasn't. Maybe she is using the Bible as a crutch. But she isn't.

We are left with the mystery of the Bible as powder keg.

Word

"I've thought of going home and pulling all the tubes out and just letting nature take its course." For someone in such desperate straits in the hospital such a reaction is entirely natural. Even though it would be suicide, one can readily be excused for thinking such thoughts.

Our job as a church at a time like this is to be there for the patient with all the presence we can muster. To be sure, we all have to do our own dying, but we do not have to do it alone. We need the love of the beloved community, as Paul called it, surrounding us as we pioneer, to use another early Christian word, the beyond. Above all, perhaps, we need the words that will carry us beyond, the metaphors, coming from the roots for "carry" and "beyond."

The church are the people who read the Bible to each other, the book of metaphors, the one that contains the words that will carry us beyond. Rarely, however, does a church member read the Bible to another member. For one thing, many church members do not know the Bible that well. For another, even if they did they would be embarrassed. It is not the way we act with one another.

Our main business as a church is to open the Bible for each other, the book of metaphors which will carry us beyond the realities of this life to those of the next. Reading the Bible, more than any other single thing the church does, is what makes a church a church. Everything else is derivative—the liturgy, the fellowship, the social action, all are secondary to the Word of God, which is so important it is capitalized and even personified—in Jesus.

The trouble with going to other members of the beloved community with the usual words is that such words are usually insufficient to carry the despairing person beyond his or her despair. "We're with you all the way." "We love you." "Be sure to call if there is anything we can do to help." Such clichés simply cannot carry the weight of bearing the other beyond. We need the words that will attach the despairing one to the Word.

One of the reasons the Bible lasts is that its metaphors work. A metaphor is what cannot be translated further. "Poetry," Robert Frost observed, "is what gets lost in translation." It is the words of Scripture that we should be carrying to the bedsides of our brothers and sisters in Christ. That is what they need. It is no accident that we call him the Living Word.

Metaphor

We were driving away from his church when he said, "The language is imprecise." He was referring to his pastor's conversation. He is a lawyer and executive of a large corporation. They are the best of friends, but their vocabularies collide.

The lawyer speaks of his profession as the bar. The pastor speaks of the bar of judgment. Both are metaphors. Both are imprecise. But both are as precise as they can be. To be more precise is to limit their effectiveness. As we have seen, if one could make the language more precise, one would.

Theology is always trying to "be more precise." But there is a limit beyond which theology cannot go. If it oversteps that limit, it may lose the truth that it is trying to communicate. The trouble with much theology is that it is written by theologians who are always trying to reduce God to "more precise" language. Some of the best theology is written by the "imprecise" poets of the the Bible. That is one of the reasons the Bible lasts. If it had been written by theologians, it would never have survived.

Still, the man's pastor has his work cut out for him. When the lawyer, using a metaphor, describes his pastor's imprecise language as "soft," it means that the pastor must make his words as "hard" as possible in order to communicate with his friend. By the same token, the lawyer must "soften" his language in order to communicate with his pastor. The lawyer knows this, of course. Otherwise he would not remain a member of the church.

It was a lawyer who asked Jesus the hard question, "Who is my neighbor?" Jesus replied with the hard story of the Good Samaritan. He adjusted metaphors. It worked.

Confirmation

A major challenge is teaching twenty eighth-graders about the Bible, God, and Jesus as well as acquainting them with the workings of the denomination and the church. Who wants to learn "all that stuff" at the age of thirteen? It presents some vexing moments.

I tried putting them in rows and teaching with a blackboard and tests. The response was swift—it was "too much like school." I would have no problem with that if I were convinced that school worked. But how much can any of us remember of what we learned in the eighth grade?

So we sat around in my office and read the Bible together. We marked the key passages in red and wrote them down at the front for quick reference. We even rewrote the passages in the teenage vernacular. I am not convinced that that approach sticks either. It all drifted away, and after the hour I was not at all sure anybody knew anything more than when they came in. I could not see that it made any difference.

So we sat around my office and talked. No Bible, no blackboard, no red pen, no notes, no homework. Just dope, sex, stealing, and then sneak in the Prodigal Son at the end. Good old inductive method. Begin with them "where they are." Deal with "the real problems of life." But I am not at all sure we are any farther along this way than we were before. Where the conversations before had drifted from the Bible, now they drifted to the Bible. And in each case I was not at all convinced that the Bible had stuck.

So now we sit around my office and I ask them questions and they teach me. Is there a God? Why Jesus? Why join the church? It drives them crazy, but we just may be learning something. I take the notes, they give the answers, and the frustration level gets so high that one week a girl cried. That was the week she shared how "stupid" she felt the whole God idea was. It was one of the best classes we ever had. It got the others sharing how they felt about the presence—and absence—of God in their lives. Then we read Job. At last it was in their blood.

Fifth Wheel

Ministers make their living with the most important thing there is—the Word of God. But ministers, like anyone else, can sometimes feel superfluous. They may get the feeling they are fifth wheels, that it is others who make the world go around. They may even feel that they are freeloaders, living off other people's earnings. A friend of mine, who belonged to a group I once ran in the local jail called "Check Writers Anonymous," used to delight in calling me a pimp.

Not long ago I visited one of my oldest friends, a man I grew up with and went to church with, the kid down the block. He is now chairman of the board of one of the large corporations in town. His secretary has a desk bigger than mine. You walk into his office and the carpet tickles your ankles. Original paintings are on the oak-panelled walls. A man is on the sofa to take notes of my friend's conversation with two executives, who are also there. My friend crowds me—the boy he used to play rounders with—into his impossible schedule and tells the others in his office how I am a minister, how I ran for mayor of a city once, wrote some books, did this and that. Suddenly he says how nice it was of me to drop by, which is obviously my cue, and you can bet your life I get out of there.

Those who can, do, to paraphrase George Bernard Shaw; those who can't, preach. The titans of industry like my old pal are out there making the decisions that affect thousands. I'm in my study with the Bible writing the sermon for Sunday. It's got to be crazy. What's even crazier is that I wouldn't be doing anything else.

Guest Room

We were visiting in the home of a couple to whom we had been close years before. The guest room was their daughter's. She had long since grown and gone. On the bottom shelf of her bookcase a book caught my eye. It was a familiar Bible, still in its red jacket, the kind I used to give the children in the third grade. I opened it. Sure enough, there was my signature and the date and the inscription from Jeremiah: " 'When you seek me with all your heart, I will be found by you,' says the Lord." The Bible had never been opened.

Doubtless this happens more often than I like to think. Clearly the fault is shared. On the one hand, it is the fault of the church. We had obviously not brought the Bible alive for her. We had not made it something she could not do without. On the other hand, the fault was hers. She had made no effort to make the book hers. The pages were clean. They had never been turned. There were no marks.

The fault is also the Bible's. It is not always easy to understand. It is out of chronological order. It is often boring. There are no subheads. One never knows where one is. It is difficult to read without reading another book at the same time which explains what is going on. Without digging, you rarely know who wrote what, to whom, under what circumstances. Let's face it, the Bible, for many, is not an inviting book.

It's different if one has been issued a personal invitation.

That is where we missed the mark. Neither her teachers nor her parents nor her friends nor I had said to her: "This is the most exciting book I have ever read. Will you let me share my excitement with you?" That is one of the few ways a young person can be lured into reading the Bible. It has to be so attractive to someone else, whom the young person likes, that the young person will give it a try.

Her father visited us not long ago. He had gotten to know a man a few blocks away. That summer the man had asked him to accompany him as he took some teenagers to church camp. My friend had accepted. He said that, for the first time in his life, he had really been reading his Bible. "Which one?" I asked. He couldn't remember the name, but he was so excited he went out to his car to get it. It was the Good News Bible. "Look," he said, "It has subheads and pictures and a paragraph at the front of each book indicating who wrote it, to whom, under what circumstances. And it's only $5.95." The next Sunday I held up the Bible in church and suggested everyone buy it.

Sadly, if my friend had been that enthusiastic about his Bible eleven years ago, his daughter might have been, too. Ditto for her teachers and friends—and me.

A Child's Bed

"When she didn't receive a kid's Bible for Christmas," her mother wrote, "she was disappointed. So, last week I got her one. She 'reads' it and does 'homework' from it every day. Sometimes I find her with her reading light on in bed 'reading' it! Isn't that wonderful?!" She is four years old.

They are clearly starting out right. "So much depends upon/ a red wheelbarrow/ glazed with rain water/ beside the white chickens," William Carlos Williams wrote. So much depends upon a child's Bible beside a child's bed. If we start reading the

Bible early we will continue reading it late. I can still see the pictures in the child's Bible my mother used to read to us. So can my brothers and sister. And they can tell you the stories, too. Indeed they are, or have, to their own children.

"Train up a child in the way he should go," the Bible says, "and when he is old he will not depart from it." Yet most of us leave our children's Bible reading to a series of well-meaning friends at Sunday school. We invest other parents with the responsibility to teach our children the Bible. It doesn't add up.

Of course, it can go the other way, too. By senior high age many young people feel the Bible was a kids' book and so is no longer for them. The same is often true in college. I did a TV program with a Christian professor of statistics at a local university. Before we went on the air he told me that only once, in all his twenty-eight years at the university, had anyone ever initiated a religious conversation with him—and the "once" was an atheist graduate student who was trying to convert him to atheism. He explained that students and faculty alike felt they had outgrown their need for God now that they were in college or graduate school.

A study was done not long ago at the University of Minnesota which indicated that a parent's religion, or lack thereof, had a great deal to do with a child's. It is a sociological statistic to give credibility, if such be needed, to the Bible's assertion, "Train up a child." Perhaps my letter-writer said it best, regarding her child. "She's my little Christian. Praise God—and pray it only grows."

Going Back

There he was. I hadn't seen him in four years. He was waiting patiently at the end of the line after church. "Wow!" I exclaimed when I saw him. He grinned. We hugged.

He had been one of those kids everyone likes. Quiet, strong, a leader. The girls were crazy about him. The boys admired him. Adults predicted a great future.

Then he moved away. And, as such things go, we drifted out of touch. I heard from him once, and he heard once from me. And then there he was on that Sunday morning as strong and quiet as ever.

We set up a time and he came over to the house. It gave me a chance to give him his Bible back. The sexton had found it when he was cleaning up. It had been left in a confirmation class long since. I could have sent it to him, of course, but I kept thinking I would see him, that he would be back to visit his friends, and then I forgot about it.

In the meantime he had gotten another. He told me about it and how he had been reading it and how it had been in his life and how the Bible had spoken to him at the right times. There had been downs as well as ups since he left, but the Bible had always been there, he said, to bring him back.

That's what the Bible does, I thought. It brings us back. No matter how far we may go, no matter how far we may fall, at the most distant place the Bible can bring us back—if, that is, we have had some knowledge of the Bible in the first place. By the same token, there are, of course, plenty of stories of people who have picked up a Gideon Bible in a motel room without ever having been to the Bible before and seen their lives brought back.

In his case it was confirmation. He had opened his Bible for the first time. It became his friend. I had looked in it before I returned it. Sure enough, it was marked at all the places we had marked in class. And, yes, there was the story of the Prodigal Son and our underlining: "When he came to himself he said, 'I will arise and go to my father'." He would go back.

And now he was here, if only briefly, back with his church, back where it had all begun, back where he had gotten not so much the knowledge as the love of the Word of God. That was it, not the knowledge but the love. It was the love that brought him back to the Bible when he needed it, just as it was the love of the young man's father that brought the Prodigal Son back. The Bible is home.

A Simple Passion

"I'm so happy you're reaching him through history," she said regarding her husband. "He went out and bought a new Bible." The Word of God is speaking to him as never before, and all because of the politics and economics, the facts and dates, of three thousand years ago.

Many different things make the Bible attractive to different people. Some will be attracted out of need. Others out of curiosity. Others out of a desire to know about Eastern culture. Others out of love of poetry. Others out of interest in politics and economics.

I know a high school English teacher who is an atheist but who insists on teaching the Bible because he considers his pupils illiterate without it. That may be overstating it a bit, but at the very least one is culturally deprived without a knowledge of the culture's basic book.

Pastors and others often wheedle, needle, and inveigle people into reading the Bible. Because once people are reading, there is no telling what might happen. The tragedy is that so few actually do read. In a given church no more than ten percent of the members will be regular readers of the Bible, let alone serious students.

We gave a little test one Sunday morning during worship. Who came first, David or Moses? Name the fifth book of the Bible. Questions like that. The average grade was a stunning twenty-six percent. Who were the Pharisees? Back came the answer: "The bad guys in black hats." What were the Epistles? "The wives of the apostles."

As with anything else, the motivation is all. Her husband could not be happier with his. For years he had been away from the Bible. Now he is back. What is the allure? A simple passion for history, a passion that he has had since grade school. He will meet his Lord through his facts.

Priorities

I sometimes wonder what my job is. One seldom does that in other professions. "Here's your job description, and here's what you do—one, two, three." I have that all right, but it can leave me guessing.

The minister is supposed to administer, for instance, but there are plenty of people who can do that. I am supposed to counsel, but there are others doing that. I represent the church in the community, but all sorts of people do that.

My job is to preach and teach. I am paid to study the Bible, something that the church members do not take time for. It might be nice if they did, of course, but "modern life" being what it is, it is not "realistic" to expect that they will. There are "only so many hours in the day." Our top-quality time goes to job and family.

My job is the Bible. It is to spend an hour of preparation for every minute in the pulpit. And it is to spend two hours of preparation for every one hour of teaching. That's the better part of a workweek right there. But that is the minister's part. Every other activity is secondary. Preaching and teaching are first.

Why? Because the Bible is first. The reason churches languish—when they do—is that the pastor's job description is awry. The people may want the pastor to be an executive and "run a tight ship." But that kind of expertise can be hired elsewhere. In a smaller church it can even be volunteered. Or they may want the pastor to be a therapist, but, again, there are other people trained to do that. Or they may want the pastor to lead the charge in social action, but the members themselves can often do that.

By the same token, human nature being what it is, the pastor may gravitate naturally to a secondary role. Because one is "relational," one ends up spending more and more time in counseling. Because one is a "hard charger," one finds oneself more and more in social action. Because one is a "nuts and bolts-er," administration begins to take over.

All such jobs are secondary. This is not to say they need not be done. It is the minister's job to see that they are, either by the minister or by the minister's getting others to do the ministering. Another reason churches languish—when they do—is that all five jobs are not being done. Again, the job description has gone awry.

The key to the enterprise is to keep first things first. When first things become second and second things first, watch out. The church is in trouble. Any minister who does not want, more than anything else, to communicate the Bible had better not be a minister.

Now, this is not to say that the Bible is not communicated through administration, counseling, and social action. Clearly it is. And if it isn't, then there is something amiss. What is meant by keeping first things first is that the minister's call is to preach and to teach. The other three are an echo. This does not mean that the echo is not heard. Indeed, it must be heard or the job description will not be met. All it means is that the echo is not the call.

Christmas Story

On Christmas Eve I went to jail to see a man whom I had seen in jails before. As such things go, I had to leave almost as soon as I arrived. They needed me at church to read the part about the child.

To let me see my friend, they had to dig him from the "Hole," where he had been for several weeks. "He fell apart," it was explained to me. Two years, six months, and thirteen days, and Number A-7850 had "snapped" and then "lashed out." "It happens," I was told.

I went through the enormous doors as each sprang shut behind. They brought him in. He blinked. I waved across the room. We talked. I asked him how he was. He said, "I'm doing fine," and laughed. It was a brazen shot. The guard looked up. Soon I left the prison for the church.

On the way back through snow that slowed me to fifty, then forty, I remembered how, while wives and children flowed through the doors to sit austerely with the men in brown, the last blue entry, other than mine, on his "Authorized Visitors Card" had been on Christmas Eve a year ago. I pulled up at the church.

Chapter 5

Worship in This Parish

Process

"I heard laughter when I came in," the visitor said after church. "I saw people hugging each other as I left. I make my living in show business, and the way we tell if we're making it in a show is if the hair stands up on the backs of our heads. Well, it was standing up on the back of mine this morning."

He said something more. "I've learned," he added, "that if you don't like what you're doing, don't do it. The process is all." If Sunday morning isn't good process, you can forget about product. If the process is right, the result will be.

One problem in churches is that we become fixated on product and so neglect process. We go for the goal when we should be going for the journey. Journey is what faith is about. "By faith, Abraham went out, not knowing where he was to go." He had no idea where he'd stop. The journey was all.

What happens is that we close the windows, turn on the air conditioning, and barrel to church. That's a worthy objective, to be sure. But we miss a lot on the way. Coming to church only for the sermon, for instance, which many do, means that you miss the rest of the service.

On the way to the goal we miss the journey. We lose the fun. And then we wonder why the budget inched up only three percent. It's because people weren't laughing and hugging each other. The hair wasn't standing up on the back of their heads.

Spontaneity

It had been one of those Sundays. A woman said that her husband would have an operation Wednesday for a brain tumor, and a man said his father's operation had been a success. Some people from one of our mission projects gave us a ham. A man asked for prayers for his brother, who had just lost his job. An elder choked up as he told how a church member much sicker than he, in a room down the hall, had come to visit him as he convalesced. A couple who had moved away were unexpectedly back. Afterwards people were talking. "Powerful," our worship chairman said, and we embraced. There were tears in his eyes.

No one can predict when worship services like this will occur. Nor can one explain what happens when they do. Neither the prediction nor the explanation, of course, is necessary. Good worship cannot always be rolled through a mimeograph. Indeed, first-century worship was so open, free, and spontaneous that it proved irresistible. "Each one has a hymn, a lesson, a revelation," Paul wrote. Something is lost when the leadership of the worship is solely in the hands of the pastor. After all, the word "liturgy" comes from two Greek words that, when combined, mean "the work of the people."

There are those, to be sure, who don't care for such spontaneity. They want their service decorous, with everything in place. As Paul also said, "All things should be done decently and in order." His stricture, however, applied to the orderly progression of events. It was not an injunction to avoid spontaneity.

A risk is involved, to be sure. The spontaneity may "get out of hand." That happens twice a year at the most. Someone will "preach." Someone will "go on too long." Someone will speak "too often." But these are risks worth running when the reward is the blessing of the Holy Spirit. As to prediction, remember, as we have seen Jesus say, "the wind blows where it wills." The best we can do is get out of the way.

That is why, when the church service slavishly follows the mimeograph, the Spirit is often cranked out as the ink is cranked on. It is safer that way. But who wants a safe service? Some do. A few have left our church for safer havens. But if Paul and company had played it safe, that early worship would never have taken hold. If they had not been open to the fresh and powerful wind of the Holy Spirit, we would not be worshiping now. The one aspect of the service visitors comment on most frequently is the time when the Spirit speaks. This is not to say that the Spirit does not speak through what is decent and orderly. It is only to say that the Spirit can also speak through what is a little "indecent" and "disorderly." Powerful worship has both.

Different

He is in church every week, his wife rarely, his children never. I wonder what draws him. I wonder what draws the others. Why do they come? They could be home with the Sunday paper, out on the golf course, fixing the faucet, paying the bills.

I imagine that it must have something to do with the words. When during the week does he use the word "God"? And the mood. When during the week does he pray? Sing? Ask ultimate questions?

In church, transcendence breaks in on immanence, the divine on the human. But what does that mean? It means that for one hour he lives in a different dimension of reality. He will then go home and see his wife and children differently.

How do you describe the difference? A woman stayed after church to talk, and there were tears in her eyes. A man called to say he had heard of another man with cancer, and he wanted to know more about him, not only about his illness but about him. A teenager called to arrange time for a coke and to ask how my day had been. All the ordinary stuff of life, to be sure. But with a difference, a hint of transcendence, of God.

When my friend goes home after his hour away, he is somehow better able to take the pain of his wife's distance and the regret of his children's being so caught in one dimension of reality they cannot see two. It is this seeing double that we call good worship.

Faces

Each Sunday begins here. I am alone in my office. It is an act that is duplicated in churches everywhere. But the pastor is never alone. As the pastor prays, the faces come.

This morning there was Nancy from nineteen years ago, and old Mrs. Brant, "the angel of the seventh floor," dying in the hospital, and Jim who was considering whether to take the new job, and my little renegade in confirmation who refused to join the church just because her parents wanted her to, and the two good men of this church who prayed with me often a year ago here.

For some reason it takes me back to a distant church where I was invited to preach the first year I was ordained. As I stood in the little room off the narthex two men walked in. It turned out they were members of the church board. "We always pray with the pastor," they explained, "before the service begins." They will never know what an impact that had. Their faces, vague now, are before me as I write.

Before church Sunday morning is a lonely time for pastors. It may be the awesomeness of the task. It may be the desire to do well. It may be anxiety about the various parts of the service. For whatever reason, the loneliness brings the faces into the office, the study, the little room off the narthex. The pastor is not alone. All these good people, past and present, are there, too, and they are saying, in effect, "We will pray with you before the service begins."

Virile

I suggested we all pray at a certain time every day, wherever we were, with whatever was on our hearts. Only three signed up after the service. All were women. The group has now expanded to nine. But there is only one other man besides me.

For some reason prayer is not considered virile. For that matter, religion is often not considered virile either. Far more women than men are in churches. It is the reverse of what it was in Jesus' time. The twelve disciples were men. The letters and journeys were virtually all by men. To be sure, there were cultural constraints against women's doing this sort of thing, and there are numerous mentions of women in the New Testament. Still, the men seem to have been praying more in the first century than they are in the twentieth.

Maybe it's genetic. Some evidence suggests that the male brain is specialized but the female brain is not. Both hemispheres in a woman's brain work on a problem. But men use the right hemisphere for spatial problems and the left for verbal. Their right does better than women's right. Men read maps and do geometry better than women. But women, using both sides of the brain at once, are better at relationships. They sense how others feel. It is their celebrated "sixth sense." Consequently, women may have a better "feel" for God. Or at least a more "natural" one in response to a request to pray.

Maybe the problem is educational. Men are taught that prayer isn't "logical." It doesn't "make sense." It isn't "scientific." Again, the reasons may be cultural, but there are fewer women in science and engineering than men. It is rare that a woman gets a Nobel Prize in chemistry or physics. Because prayer is not "physical" or capable of chemical analysis, it is, at least initially, perhaps less "natural" for men.

Maybe the reason is emotional. Men are supposed to "control their emotions." Boys are told not to cry. It isn't masculine to show emotion, and prayer can be emotional. Indeed, prayer will be emotional if it is done right. Our relationship with God will affect us that deeply. If that is the case, then the reason men are reluctant to pray is that they are afraid. They are afraid to "show emotion." They are afraid they will "let things get out of hand." They are afraid of "what people might think" if someone saw them with their heads in their hands.

Whatever the reason, I was elated when a man said he

wanted to join us. To top it off, he is a master of the left brain—
an accountant. Just as there was a Madame Curie who knew
about radium, so there is a CPA who knows about prayer. When
asked what field held the greatest hope for future research, the
renowned inventor, Charles Steinmetz, said: "Prayer—find out
about prayer."

Wrestling

"It's a strange feeling," he said as he prayed, "wrestling with
the one I'm trying to love." Others agreed. You could hear it
under their breaths. He had struck a chord. By the one he loved
he meant God, not his wife. He is an executive of a large
corporation. He is responsible for many people.

I have heard him pray like this before. His prayers are always
short and labored. He falters, as he rarely does in business. I have
an idea such faltering is good for him. He is getting in touch with
a lost part of himself. It is getting in touch with him.

He calls it wrestling. That's all right, of course, because it's
manly. But unbeknownst to him, there's more to it than that. It
goes all the way back. Jacob wrestled with God on the banks of
the River Jabbok. My friend is a modern Jacob. The story is as
old as it is new. It is the age-old story of trying to find peace with
God.

I have an idea such peace is on its way for my friend. It is
coming through his struggle. His struggle is the submerged part of
himself emerging. God is coming into view. Prayer is letting God
emerge.

The trouble, of course, is that most of us will do anything to
avoid such struggle. It is too painful to have the repressed
expressed. So we do everything to prevent being found by what
we have lost. And that is why the peace of God escapes us. We
refuse to be saved by the very thing that can save us. And that,
too, is an old story. It is summarized best on a cross.

So when my friend wrestles, everyone in the room knows, in the depths of his or her being, in the silence, listening to him, that God is moving into view.

Scream

We had finished praying in the sanctuary, a small group of us, when a man asked, "Has anybody ever screamed in here?" He has suffered a business reverse, and his wife has a difficult illness. It reminds one of the psalmists. Of Job. Of everyone who ever wanted to express how he or she felt in a church.

We don't do that much. And when we do, we channel our feelings into harmony and let the choir sing our feelings for us. Even the hymns, which the whole congregation sings, advance measure by measure. And they are fine, make no mistake. There are few things more emotional than lusty singing on Sunday morning.

But we miss the screams. The person beside us in the pew could be dying, and we would never know it. That is why we open the service for a few minutes each week. Last Sunday a man talked about his son on drugs. A woman asked for help with her excruciating back. A grandfather said how he and his wife were taking care of their grandchildren while the parents were gone for a week because of the ill health of the mother, their daughter.

What do you get in a church that you don't get anywhere else? The chance to share how you feel? The man talking about his son on drugs went on to talk about the school system and how ineffective it was when it came to drugs. A woman one Sunday talked about how ineffective she felt most of us were because we were putting "prayer and Bible reading" ahead of "social action." A man shared every week for four weeks the progress of his dying friend.

Would life be any different without churches? Without this people, this parish we might never hear the screams. We might not even hear the groans. We would be so intent on pursuing our own lives that we would be out of touch with the rest of life. Churches give us perspective. They keep us in touch with "reality." A nine-to-five day at the office and home to the spouse and kids is unrealistic. Churches won't let us get away with avoiding "life."

So who wants to get up on Sunday morning for that? About a billion people.

Crisis

He stood up during the open time in the service to say they were leaving the area. He started to say how much this people, this parish had meant to him, but he couldn't get through. So he sat down, saying simply, "Thank you."

It is amazing how much people's churches come to mean to them. In his case the church had meant little for years. Then, as often happens, he came on hard times in his business and family life. We began to meet regularly. He reached out to others in the church. They reached out to him. He has not been the same since.

Nor have we. It is always two-way. He who had been with us so long did not know us. But we who had been with him as long did not know him either. It was the crisis that brought him back. No cross—no Christ; no crisis—no Christian. It took a disruption of his carefully planned existence to bring us back to each other.

It should not have to be that way. We should be as attuned to each other in the high and midpoints of life as well as the low. But the harmonies to which churches resonate do not always reveal the high and mid-notes without the low. We do not always know how much we need the church until our lives have been disrupted.

Jesus disrupted people's lives. Things were fine for Peter in his fishing business, we can assume. Then Jesus came into his life. There are virtually no instances in all the stories about Jesus of people becoming believers in him without some form of disruption occurring in their lives. And if they were not already disrupted, as with illness, he caused disruption, as with his calls to the disciples and his challenges to the Pharisees.

So when my friend stood up and started to say how much we had meant to him, we understood why he couldn't get through. Some of us weren't doing so well either. It was not only that he and his wife were moving away. It was a reminder to all of us how much we needed each other. And we knew once again that it is only the ground disrupted by the plow that yields the crop.

Communion

I took the communion on Maundy Thursday to the sick and shut-in. They were grateful, of course, but I don't know how much it meant. There is not much sense of communion among many Protestants. Episcopalians and Lutherans have it, but many other Protestants do not. At best it is celebrated; at worst, tolerated.

I have always wondered why this is so. Communion is one of the two "dominical" sacraments, those instituted by the Lord, the "dominus." The other is baptism. Clearly, what happened that first Maundy Thursday was compelling in its simplicity and imminent doom. That a man could take the basic elements of a meal, bread and wine, and make something significant out of them for the next two thousand years was remarkable.

Still, many Protestants balk. "It's communion again," they

say on arriving at church. They feel cheated out of a full-length sermon. Why the emphasis on the word over the sacrament escapes me. But I have a hunch it is because many Protestants, at least in the Reformed tradition, tend to be rationalists. They feel safer thinking about concepts than sharing experiences.

For one thing, the meal is not really a meal, only a symbol of a meal. Many people have trouble with symbols. The American flag is one thing, but a crumb of bread and a thimble of wine are quite another. In this case, it is hard to see beyond the visible. It is hard to get back to that first Maundy Thursday and imagine oneself in the presence of Jesus.

For another thing, the bread and the wine mysteriously convey the body and blood of Christ, and rationalists have a problem with mystery. They want it explained, and if they can't explain it they are likely to leave it to others who think they can. They tend to back away from it with such pejoratives as "mystical" and "unrealistic."

What the communion does is enable us to see beyond the visible. And when I walked into the first home and placed the communion set on the table and said the words and broke the bread and poured the wine, there was a distant look in the quiet eyes of the elderly couple. Perhaps they were remembering prior communions shared with this people, this parish. Perhaps they were remembering communions long ago with their parents. Who knows? Who is to say? What is important is that their distant look suggested that they had heard beyond words and seen beyond sight. It is quite possible the communion meant far more to them than I thought.

Ceremony

They moved into their new home, and some thirty of us were standing around their living room. He asked me to pray. It was a "house blessing." Remarkably, there have been others. It is a new phenomenon. More accurately, it is an old one coming back.

Such ceremonies were frequent when life was viewed as religious. The Ojibwa had a ceremony for opening the wild rice season. We still open many public meetings with prayer. Families remember God daily around the table. But that is about it these days. The ceremonial aspects of life are vanishing, unless, that is, such ceremonies as house blessings can bring them back.

It all depends on one's ability to think in one dimension while living in another. The Ojibwa saw beyond the wild rice to God. Ironically, those who were "bringing God to the Indian" were those who were tearing up the rice beds with their log-floats. One does not read of religious ceremonies in logging camps. The Ojibwa, on the other hand, were able to see one thing in terms of another. That is why so much American Indian art, largely undiscovered, is so rich.

When a baby is born, there is a celebration, but is there a ceremony? When a husband or wife gets a promotion, there is a celebration, but is there a ceremony? When a child graduates, the family moves, someone is ill—all are times for ceremony. The word comes from the Latin for "religious rite." But we have limited ceremony to one morning or evening a week, and for the one-third of American Protestants, one-fourth of American Jews, and three-fifths of American Catholics who participate, that is pretty much it, although many Jews have a weekly ceremony in the home as well.

What we have lost is our ability to think theologically, to see God in wild rice. "The struggle continues in the living room," Kierkegaard said. He was right on the mark. That is why the one ceremony in which people do participate each week, no matter what the percentages, has to be so powerful that it rockets people out of there to conduct other ceremonies on other days. We now have some thirty people who bow their heads at nine every morning, wherever they are, to remember God in their lives. It is a modest ceremony, to be sure, but it is gaining in impact. Reports are coming in that it is putting the divine dimension into people's days. That, of course, is just what ceremony is for.

Attendance

She almost never comes to church, and yet at Christmas there is always a substantial gift and note. This year she wrote: "Again, I would like to say thanks to the Lord for the many years his teachings have been a guide in my business as well as personal life. The church *is* our foundation."

She is immensely successful, highly respected, and does very well without the church. It is the Abraham Lincoln syndrome. He never joined a church, rarely attended, and is widely viewed as one of our most religious Americans. If people like my friend and Abraham Lincoln can be good Christians without the church, why the church?

One cannot argue such things. One can only speak for oneself. Most people in churches find they are in them because they cannot stay out of them. They cannot be "good Christians" apart from their church. There is too much going on there that they need—the singing and praying, the Bible, each other.

Most of us need all the help we can get to live in the fourth dimension. That is why the church lasts. Psychology, sociology, and ecology—those are the easy dimensions. But theology? We all live in relation to self, others, world. But we do not all live in relation to God, at least not as naturally as in the other three. We need music, Scripture, other people to transport us there.

I grew up in the church Lincoln sometimes attended. The presidential pew was in front, with the ropes and the cellophane and the two little flags, one for the country and one for the presidency. It wasn't until later that I learned he rarely used the pew. Not that he had anything against church, he explained. It just wasn't for him.

A friend of evangelist Dwight L. Moody visited Moody one night. He told Moody he felt he could be a "perfectly good Christian" without going to church. In response, Moody said nothing. Instead, he reached forward to the fireplace with the tongs, withdrew a coal, and held it up to his friend. It died.

Kleenex

"It was a snowstorm of Kleenex," she said after the service of confirmation. Her own daughter had been in the group, and she and the other parents had been visibly moved.

But so had others in the congregation. There was a sense in which they were all our daughters and all our sons. From the very beginning at their baptisms, when their parents had taken a vow to bring them up "in the nurture and admonition of the Lord," they had become ours as well as theirs. For we too took a vow, to stand behind their parents in providing for their education as young Christians. And now they were all here, in this service of confirmation, the climax of their years in church school.

The climax, yes, but not the end. Hopefully the service is just a beginning. "I am still learning" was Michelangelo's motto. They have come so far and learned so much in order to go even farther and learn even more. At least that is the theory. Occasionally one or another confirmand will vanish after the service. We will call. We will send the other kids over. We will even "kidnap," surprising the vanished new church member at home and bringing him or her to the youth group. But it rarely works.

The reason it rarely works is that the parents have often vanished, too. "What is the best way to bring up a child?" Albert Schweitzer was asked. "There are three ways," he replied. "By example, by example, and by example." When teenagers have no example of the importance of a church family behind their own family, their dropping out can, almost without fail, be predicted.

However, we don't give up. It is quite possible that a parent will be active and a child not. That is the other side of the coin. With smashing success a fifteen-year-old went up to another at high school and said, "I am on a mission from God. God wants you at youth group." It was brash, all right, but it took. One reason it took is that there was already parental involvement.

I am reminded of the power such a witness can have. The

great religious leader, Thomas Merton, during his atheist days at Columbia University dropped in on a church service. He happened to sit next to a fifteen-year-old girl who was praying. She was praying so simply and yet so ardently that he was moved one step further toward accepting the call that had been working in him to give his life to Christ.

One reason the Kleenex was out at the service is that others in the church family were remembering their calls to give their lives, too, to Christ.

Wedding

You pause at the back with your dad, and then you begin the walk down the aisle. The people are standing. The trumpet and organ are playing. You and your dad are smiling, confident, sure.

I think of other weddings I have done as you walk toward me, and I think how good yours is. It is somehow in that confidence you show as you lean lightly on your father's arm. Not every bride has that.

I first experienced this good feeling in our times together before today. You remember how you would come to my office and we would talk about who you were and how you saw yourself and how you saw yourself with your husband-to-be. And he would be there, too, and the talk would turn to him.

Now he is here. He steps forward to take your other arm, and there you are, with him on your right and your dad on your left, and you are looking up at me, still smiling, and beyond me to the ten-foot cross nailed to the wall behind me.

It is as though your love were a reminder to all of us of God's. That is why you have come to the church to be married. Behind the dresses and evening clothes and flowers, we are here for God as well as for you, and I sense you sense that.

You move a half-step in, your attendants just behind. They too turn in, their eyes on you, then me, then on the wall beyond. I have no idea what their religions are, but I close my eyes and ask that your being here, with your two strong men beside you, may somehow serve to bring Christ down from his cross for all who are with you here.

I nod to your mother, the congregation sits, and we begin.

Gregorian Chant

Often I hear a Gregorian Chant. It comes at unusual times. I am on an airplane at the moment, and there it is. Nobody else hears it, of course. "Dies irae, dies illa." No, I do not think it is my "return to Rome," as my Catholic friends like to joke. Nor do I think it is a return to "the old, traditional ways." But I do think it is a return to a deep part of myself.

Religion comes from the Latin for "bind back." And the chant when it comes is "tolling me back . . . to my sole self," as Keats put it. I remember standing at his grave in Rome. "Here lies one whose name is writ in water." Before my name is writ in water there are depths I'd like to explore. There are depths exploring me. The Gregorian Chant when it comes is my Siren.

Unfortunately, the Sirens called sailors to their doom, and I resist going into my unexplored depths. Fear is as good a rationalization as any to stay on the surface when the song comes. But I guess that is not to be. The minister is drawn into the depths. Something is calling.

The rewards, of course, outweigh the risk. The saints all risked the journey down. That's why they were saints. Clearly I am not in their category, but it does appear that of this people, this parish, I am the one who is called to take that journey for all of us. No, that is not saying it right. We are all called. It is the priesthood of all believers. What pastors are called to do is model the call, take the risk, go down, for all to see, into their unexplored depths—in prayer, meditation, dream, Bible, and inner conversations where they may feel least comfortable. This is how we are "bound back" to the rest of who we are.

I don't suppose Paul was particularly comfortable going back to his friends and telling them he had turned Christian. Or that the disciples were particularly comfortable as they "turned the world upside down." They were risking death. But it was for the sake of life, of being bound back to all of who they were. No, this is not masochism. It is realism. If we are ever going to be real, we must risk listening to "the still, small voice" within, the Gregorian Chant, whatever it is that is calling us back to our sole self. Because that is God.

Holy

It had been a devastating moment in her life when one of her most important projects had failed. I called her at her office and offered to pray with her on the phone. She accepted readily. Later her husband told me she had called him and reported "the load had been lifted."

If worship were confined to the sanctuaries, it would never have made it out of the first century. Indeed, in the first century there were no Christian sanctuaries. Maybe that is one reason the worship was so powerful.

Somewhere along the line, the vast majority of Christians got the idea that worship was what went on within the four walls of a church. Clearly it is, but it can go on elsewhere as well. Some of the best worship goes on outside the walls. God came to Moses, the Bible says, "outside the camp."

One of my most powerful worship experiences was on a hillside in the ninth grade. It was at night, which helped. Each worshiper had a candle, which also helped. We were symbolizing the light of the world; we were impressionable, and it had nothing to do with "church." The singing was unbelievable. So was the silence.

I was with an infrequent church attender at his hospital bed. He told me afterwards that more had been accomplished there than in many weeks of church. That may reflect on him as well as on the vitality of our worship, but still, if we can get people out of the norm, the abnormal can lift the veil from God as perhaps nothing else.

At last we are getting wise and sponsoring more retreats. They are actually advances in getting close to God. One of their most distinctive aspects is worship in an unfamiliar setting and in unfamiliar ways. My wife and I sat under the trees in northern Wisconsin last week and experienced a service that was a superb purveyor of the holy.

That's an interesting word, "holy." Its basic meaning in Hebrew is "distance." Maybe we are too close in our churches. Maybe they are too familiar. Not always, of course, but often. We get too comfortable in that comfortable pew. There is a separation between us and God that inspires awe, that we can only bow before, and that is good for us to experience because it reminds us that we are not in control, God is.

As I looked up at the trees towering above the Bible reader last Sunday, I felt that sense of distance. Maybe that is why, too, the prayer with my friend over the telephone seemed to work. We "connected," but it was over a distance, and it was away from church and Sunday and the familiar.

Retreat

Occasionally a pastor goes away, to lead a retreat for another church, make a speech, give a sermon. Flying back now, I think of the man and his wife whose son had just been killed in a car accident three weeks before his wedding. I think of the lonely woman in back as the retreat ended, not getting up with the others. I think of the young pastor in pinstripes telling me over coffee about his church.

When it was over, I was presented with two posters they had all signed on the back. One was of people climbing a mountain as an analogue of life. The other was of an English sheep dog with hair over its eyes and the inscription, "I see with my heart."

At the end of each retreat I ask those who attended to evaluate my effectiveness. A few sentences, signed or unsigned, as they wish. "Give me a grade if you like," I say. "It's your chance to get back at all the teachers who ever graded you." And they do. Most are signed. Occasionally an unsigned one will give me a good sock to the jaw.

I will never see them again. At the beginning I say that I hope we will continue our relationship somehow. I say it again at the end. The letters come the first week or two after, then years of silence. The man and his wife go home with their grief. The lonely woman in back returns to the back row of her church. And the young pastor comes and goes in his pinstripes.

In the connecting airport in Cleveland I pick up a yellow leaf fallen from a green tree. I have been a leaf on the soil of their lives. I cannot even say a seed, an acorn. It is that evanescent. I come. I go. They came. They went. But as I passed the leaf on the airport floor, I hesitated, struck by the incongruity of it. A yellow leaf on an airport floor? For a moment, a weekend, we hesitated, struck by the incongruity of being in each other's lives. And somehow, it was beautiful.

Chapter 6

Sermons in This Parish

Letter

It was one of those Sundays. The day was bleak. Attendance was down. The sermon had bombed. It was going so poorly I cut the rest of the humor I had intended to use. A few days later I found a letter on my desk: "This is just to say that I thought your sermon on the abundant life was one of the best I have ever heard. Everyone in the congregation was in rapt attention. Just the right balance of message, drama, and humor."

Pastors can be their own severest critics. But they would do well to be chary of such self-judgments. As with one's tendency to judge others, it would be better to let God do the judging. The fact is, I was being used by God more than I knew.

"Easy on others, hard on self" is a helpful bromide, but it can be overdone. For some reason the pastorate tends to encourage self-criticism. Perhaps it is a heightened awareness of sin. Isaiah was a priest, and the realization of God in his life came as he confessed that he was a "man of unclean lips." Pastors have a healthy dose of self-awareness. Perhaps too healthy.

They also tend to have high standards. After all, they are employed by one whose standards are the highest, and it is naturally hard to measure up. In such circles no sermon ever quite makes it. We are forever "missing the mark," which is the root of the New Testament word for sin.

On the other hand, Jesus issued his counsels of perfection in order to relieve us of thinking that we could be perfect. When he said "Be ye therefore perfect," he knew that it was impossible and that if we were even going to approximate his injunction, it would have to be God who would do it. The point of the high standards is that they get us to rely not on ourselves but on God.

An early preacher discovered that when as a Pharisee he relied on himself, he failed. When as a Christian he relied on

God, he succeeded. In other words, God can turn what appears to be failure into success. Indeed, the more we appear to ourselves to fail, the more it is possible we can succeed. "My power," Paul heard God saying, "is made perfect in weakness."

My friend's letter put me back in touch with the mainstream of early preachers.

Church Board

"It was the best sermon I've ever heard," a man said coming out of church. "I didn't understand a word of the sermon today," said another, "and I'm glad I didn't. If I had I would have been depressed."

You never know how what you say is going to be received. It is just as well. If you did, it would distort everything you were trying to say. The one thing a preacher has no business doing is preaching what will be liked and avoiding what will not.

Each week it is the preacher alone with the Bible. It is what comes out of the preacher's aloneness that counts. Unfortunately, the qualities that make for aloneness are not always the qualities found in preachers. They are as gregarious as the next person. More to the point, they are as other-directed.

The trouble is that the image of God collides with the image of the church board. One stays away from controversy because Mrs. Jones, who is the largest contributor, doesn't like controversy. One refrains from intellectual depth because it puts the local banker to sleep. One shies from emotional honesty because the lay leader is embarrassed by people who share their feelings.

So when the minister is preparing the sermon, the image of God must do battle with the image of the church board. It is Jacob on the banks of the Jabbok again, wrestling with whether he will be emotionally honest with his brother the next day, as he knew God wanted him to be. Admittedly, the preacher's is a modest Jabbok, but an important one. Without such weekly wrestling the preacher lapses into cliché, which offends no one and bores everyone. I have rarely heard a sermon while on vacation that was not boring. It is a decisive factor in keeping people out of churches.

How, then, to go to the mat with God? The preacher prays long before preaching. To pray is to see God in charge of the church board. It is to see God *before* one sees the church board. It is to see God *more* than one sees the church board. If the minister cannot do that, then the minister is not in the best position to preach. Rather than Jacob at the Jabbok, preaching without praying is like Jacob's stealing his brother's birthright. He was not imaginative enough to see his brother as a child of God. The timid preacher steals the Bible from the congregation. Such a preacher sees them only as church members or board members and not as children of God.

The best sermons will always be those that some like and some don't.

Term Paper

People say they wouldn't have this job for anything. "Writing sermons," they say, "are you out of your mind? That's like writing a term paper every week. What are you, a masochist or something?"

Other people say they wouldn't have any other job. "A sermon a week," they say. "What an opportunity! You're given a chunk of time to think about the world's greatest subject matter. There's nothing bigger than God."

Every week you open the Bible. That's where it begins. You get the lesson, or reading, from the series of readings prescribed by Catholics and Protestants around the world. The idea is to hit the major themes of the Bible in three-year cycles. Or you get the reading from the curriculum used in the church school. Or you get it from your own head and heart.

Then it's you and the Bible. You let the words work their way through you. Later you pull the books from the shelves to see what the scholars have said. Everything you do that week works its way in and out of those words. You are weaving a tapestry. "The figure a poem makes," Robert Frost said. It is being woven for you across the warp and woof of your life.

You write down everything that comes to you as you reflect on the words and your week. Sometimes I will use an entire pad of 8 1/2 x 11 paper. You put your papers in piles—so many for point one, so many for points two and three. Or, if it's a one-point sermon, you have a couple of subpoints. In twenty minutes on a person's day off, the human brain has trouble listening to more than three points. And those who do the preaching have a hard time trying to come up with more than three and still be engaging.

Then the sermon writes itself. Note that it is written. The minute a preacher stops writing sermons you can tell. They come out as cliché. Approximately ninety-five percent of the preaching in America is cliché. But when you've got a preacher who is in the five percent, look out! That preacher can change your life.

How is it done? By chipping away the cliché that has barnacled the Bible for centuries. The preacher is a chiseler. The reason the Bible lies unopened in homes is that it is encrusted with words like "love," "joy," and "peace," which have long since lost their meaning through overuse. What the preacher does is chisel them back to their hulls.

"It seems to me," an astronomer is reported to have said to a preacher, "that the Bible can basically be boiled down to 'Do unto others as you would have others do unto you'." That's cliché. The preacher is said to have replied: "It seems to me that astronomy can basically be boiled down to 'Twinkle, twinkle, little star'."

The minister as chiseler wields an important tool in the construction of faith. As an ancient preacher put it to a first-century church: "The word of God is living and active, sharper than any two-edged sword, piercing to the division of marrow and spirit, and discerning the thoughts and intentions of the heart." With words like those to work their way through you every week, most preachers would say that they are paid to do what they'd pay to do.

Exam

"Preaching is like taking an exam every week," someone said. The difference is you have several hundred graders rather than one. It's a big difference. If they grade you low, it begins to show. Attendance drops. In college if you get a low grade, you can recoup your loss. In the parish, they may not come back.

In the Reformed tradition the Word became paramount. It was the Bible that gave Martin Luther his arguments. In a Reformed church you will rarely miss an open Bible at the front of the church, on the communion table or pulpit.

Because the Word was important, words began to be. The words about the Word became the most significant part of the service. Sermons would last for remarkable lengths of time. People would even go from one sermon to another.

Today people still say, "As far as I'm concerned, you can cut out the rest of the service." To be sure, that indicates a lack of education regarding the rest of the service. But it also indicates that they want to be intellectually engaged and that, until they are intellectually engaged, it may be hard for them to be spiritually engaged.

It is the Reformation "heresy." A heresy is an overemphasis on one aspect of the truth. The Reformers tended to overemphasize the intellectual at the expense of the emotional and volitional. All three are needed. All three are what got the gospel around the world. We not only study, the first church's *didache*; we also share and serve, the first church's *koinonia* and *diakonia*. Without all three we have a truncated gospel.

Still, churches are known by how they attract people to experience the whole gospel for the whole person. In the Reformed tradition you will be attracted to the church by the preaching. In the pietist tradition, you will be attracted by the emotion. And in the so-called liberal tradition, you will be attracted by the social action. To be sure, the three overlap, and in the best churches they *will* overlap. But the fact remains that a potential parishioner is first attracted by head, heart, or hand.

In my community, they tend to be attracted by the head, so I have to write a good exam every week. It can get to you after a while. Unlike the college exam, you have to be witty enough to keep people awake and incendiary enough to set them on fire. It can't always be done. No wonder Woodrow Wilson once observed, "Proof of the divinity of the gospel is all the preaching it has survived."

Self-Disclosure

I took my typewriter to be fixed, and it changed my preaching style. Without my trusty typewriter for two weeks I had to make do with whatever I could find. I hauled out the thirty-year-old desk model somebody gave to the church. The type size and spacing were different. It threw everything off. I even had to use different paper.

I found myself becoming more anecdotal, less intellectual. I was also more expansive, less compressed. For some reason I began to talk about myself, something I had rarely done before. But with that big old Royal in front of me, I found myself disclosing myself—and not just the good but the bad. It was risky, all right, but it felt good.

The response has been tremendous. It is hard to explain. The best thing I can come up with is that congregations want the person up there to be real. Sure, they want the Word to be preached, but they want it preached through the only medium we have, our own brokenness.

It seems people relate better to someone who isn't "perfect," as ministers are often perceived. Paul said he was the least of the apostles. When we confess our sins to one another, James wrote, then we are healed. When you share your strengths with me, sometimes I become afraid or competitive. But when you come to me in your weakness, often you open me to come to you in mine. That is why Jesus "emptied himself," Paul wrote, "taking the form of a servant."

My typewriter is fixed now. I haven't used it in six months.

Theology

Four people in the last four years have talked to me in depth about my sermons. The first took me to lunch, the other three wrote letters. Two were constructively critical. One was corrective of two misstatements of fact. And one was frankly perplexed.

An average of one gratuitous conversation a year about what is going on in the Bible is hardly encouraging. To be sure, one has such conversations in Bible classes and counseling sessions. But the gratuitous conversation, at someone else's initiative, outside the usual church-structures, is rare.

People in parishes need to talk to each other more about God. We need more theological conversations; in order to better understand God, we need something more arresting than twenty-minute homilies.

One way to do so is to structure conversation after the sermon. But that is not as easy as it may sound. For one thing, the next hour on Sunday morning is often scheduled for education or fellowship. For another, the sermon may need to stand on its own. It is one person's understanding of revelation at a given time in his or her life, and perhaps it should be left to stand as such. Conversation too soon may distract.

We tried "feedback" immediately after the sermon, and it was all right for a while, but gradually it petered out. People began to realize, among other things, that the timing was not right. You don't listen to Beethoven's Fifth and then sit around with the orchestra and pick it apart, no matter how constructive your comments. Yes, it is the rare sermon that even remotely approaches the caliber of Beethoven's Fifth. But it is the moment that matters more than the caliber—the moment of beauty with the symphony and the moment of truth, however garbled, with the sermon.

Another way to talk to each other more about God is simply to talk to each other more about God. It seems anomalous that people in churches do seldom what they are supposed to do most. I got a surprise, though, the other night as I said good-by to a man on the phone. He said, "God bless you." It was clearly not a theological conversation, but, equally clear, it was a theological invitation. Perhaps it is the pastor's job, more than anyone else's, to follow up such invitations. They are being issued all the time, and if there is a lack of theological conversation in a parish, one reason may be that the pastor is not following up such leads.

Authentic

You come across an old sermon, and it is so bad you wonder how the people ever put up with it. That, of course, is discouraging enough in itself. But when you think that the same thing may be going on now, your despondency goes up a notch. If I felt reasonably good about what I was doing then and it turned out the way it did, what I am doing now may well be turning out equally bad.

Preachers reflect on what they may be inflicting. It is one thing to say we are all saved by grace and so excuse a poor performance. It is another thing to know you've given a sermon your best, only to come across it a few years later and realize how feeble it actually was.

However, as suggested above, the preacher's best critic is not necessarily the preacher. Things have a way of improving. Even if they haven't, preaching is as much a testimony to the resilience of the congregation as it is to the growth of the preacher. If you are ever hard up for an example of corporate love, just walk into the nearest church while the sermon is going on.

There is an exit from such discouragement. If the sermon is authentic, if it is true to the Bible and to who the preacher is when it is given, that is all that matters. If you aren't what you were, that is to be expected. It does not invalidate what you did—if what you did sprang from who you were. If we say who we are in a sermon, what more could anyone ask? Churches are people who let each other be who they are. The preacher models that.

Books

There must be a thousand books in my church office and another thousand in my office at home. I've gone into ministers' studies all over the country, and in each of them there is a ton of books. Remarkably, many if not most of them will have been read.

I used to think books were all-important. I would spend every morning closeted with them, working on putting something together for Sunday. They are helpful, make no mistake, as far as they go. Most sermons I have heard could scarcely be said to grip the mind. The pastor didn't do the necessary homework.

But a problem for preachers is gripping the heart as well as the head. That sounds simplistic, but consider. When you get your homilies from books, you may be stirring people to think but not to feel. In other words, while you get them to consider significant thoughts, you may not engage them in significant feelings. That is why "emotional" Nazarenes and Pentecostals tithe while "intellectual" Presbyterians and Episcopalians tip. The per capita giving of Nazarenes is three times that of Episcopalians.

So I am less glued to my books at the moment. The main one I use, other than the Bible, is my datebook. I look back through what I have done, through where I have been and what I have thought and felt, to see if there is any possibility of God in it. When you read the Bible in terms of what you have done that week, rather than in terms of what someone else may have thought about the Bible, it makes a difference.

This is not to say that one does not go to the scholars; one does, but gingerly. Instead of beginning with the scholars, I now begin with myself. Instead of reading the books on the shelves and then dipping into the book of my life, I read the book of my life and then dip into the books on the shelves. This putting of horse before cart catches feeling up to thinking and moves me to act. Whether it moves anybody else is, of course, another matter. But if preachers are caught up in what they are saying and are presenting it in a provocative manner, the chances are better than even that what is said will be moving. The sermons in the Bible—from the prophets to Jesus to Paul—moved mountains, in Jesus' metaphor. Good preaching is always a moving experience.

Story

We were out the other night and our host said something about not bringing his Bible to church anymore. The implication was that the sermons were no longer biblical. If you want to get your preacher's attention, this is one way to do it. My friend is a good man. It wasn't a put-down. But it was a dig. I got the point.

The toughest line that preachers walk is between being biblical and being personal. If they overdo the one, they are not "relevant." And if they overdo the other, it is not "the gospel." The only way out is to do both. All that preachers have is their own story, told within the context of their people, their parish. And all the preacher can do is get up there on Sunday mornings and tell it within the framework of the larger story. If the preacher tells the biblical story only, it's lecturing. If the preacher tells the personal story only, it's confessing. If the preacher does both, it's preaching. There are too few preachers.

It's all in the weaving of the two stories. There are plenty of people who can get up there and give you the biblical data. An equal number can tell you about themselves. The point is to write the two stories at once. It's the old play-within-the-play idea. On top of that, the preacher has to be actor, producer, and director, as well as playwright. Good preaching is good drama.

My friend was there the following Sunday, following along in his Bible.

Vulnerability

"You are the anchor," he said. "If you show too much vulnerability their faith will collapse." He was speaking of my occasional candor in sermons about my own weaknesses and doubts. He may be right. People want to see strength up there on Sunday morning. They want a big person in a black robe assuring them that "God's in his heaven, all's right with the world." After all, that's what they come for. That's what they pay for. The preacher, of all people in the parish, is the one with the answers.

I'm not so sure. For one thing, it isn't honest. There isn't a minister, priest, or rabbi anywhere who has all the answers. Those who say they have are at best misguided and at worst demagogic. No system can comprehend God. God, by definition, is beyond comprehension. The "hidden God" of Isaiah can do things that defy explanation.

104

For another thing, being invulnerable is being inhuman. "Who is weak, and I am not weak?" Paul asked. And he was a saint. This people, this parish does not want a hero up there on Sunday morning. They do not want someone beyond belief. They want someone who has joys and sorrows similar to theirs, who hurts as they hurt. That was the point of the Incarnation. God became vulnerable. Jesus hungered, thirsted, died. His suffering hurt God. But it worked. It gave us a person we could relate to. It gave us a God who cried.

"Every time I came to church," a woman said who later joined, "I went away crying. I knew there was a whole new area of my life I wanted to explore." Our tears of joy and sadness are signs of moving into a new dimension of who we are, where we are vulnerable, where we do not have all the answers, where we are not in control. All those negatives can start adding up to God. It is the ancient "via negativa," or negative way, to God. We are not in control; God is. We do not have all the answers; God has. Where we are most vulnerable, God is most possible. What people need to see up there on Sunday morning is someone who has the strength to be weak.

Maybe that is why another man said to me excitedly over the phone, "I come to Thursday and realize Sunday is only three days away."

Wave of Salvation

"I felt profoundly touched that you would tell our story, that your prayers for us and those of fellow believers were heard by the Lord who *called us back* eight years ago! I felt a huge wave of *salvation* sweep over me as you spoke and the hot, grateful tears on my cheeks testified to the grace in my life. What an incredible gift!"

It was a heartfelt letter after the Sunday sermon, complete

with underlinings. What a story hers is! How they were away from church for years and how eventually they came back and how their lives have not been the same since. Nor have ours, for they have touched countless numbers of us with their witnessing and care.

What happened? She put her finger on it when she wrote of those who were praying for them, even those in their own family. There was no concerted effort, no organized attack to get them back. Apparently a person here, another there, would pray and eventually they returned. Cause and effect? Who's to say? It is enough that she reads it that way.

She also put her finger on it when she wrote of grace. She knew it was grace because of her tears. They were its evidence. We need a lot more such evidence in churches. This is not to say that emotion is the only evidence of grace. Witness the "Angelic Doctor," Thomas Aquinas, and all the other great theologians. It is only to say that emotion is *also* an evidence of grace, as well as intellect, and that it is all too often lacking in churches.

I was invited to give the Alumni Day address at my seminary a few years back. I complimented the faculty on the fine education we had received, but I suggested there was one glaring lacuna, or gap. We had failed to educate the heart. We knew all about God in our heads, but we had failed to experience God in our hearts. Not all of us to be sure, but enough of us to make it worth an Alumni Day address.

I realize that the timeworn distinction between head and heart can be futile. But one of the reasons it is timeworn is that it works. We can know all about God intellectually, but until we have known God emotionally, we have not *known* God. We have not experienced grace. We have not been saved.

She put her finger on it when she wrote of salvation. "I felt a huge wave of salvation sweep over me," and then she underlined that big word. She is as bright as the next person and knows as much about God as any of us, but it wasn't until she experienced God, until she had been called back, that the "hot, grateful tears" could come.

It was all in the coming back, as the boy with his Bible. Without this people, this parish, she might never have received her "incredible gift." "Thanks be to God," Paul wrote, "for his inexpressible gift!" He was referring to Christ. Without this people, this parish, she might never have met her Lord and Savior. I was glad I had told her story.

About-Face

"You just saved me two thousand dollars," she said after the service. The sermon had been on Ahab and the neglect of the poor by the rich. She said she was going to give the money she had been saving for furniture to those who had none, not even a bed.

The Word can do this to you. It has been delivering this kind of about-face for centuries. One is reminded of a dissolute Augustine, who heard a child's voice coming from a neighboring house. "Tolle, lege," it kept repeating, "Take up [and] read." He understood it to be God's command to him to pick up his Bible and read the first passage upon which his eyes would fall. He did just that. His eyes fell on Romans 13:13–14.

> Let us then cast off the works of darkness and put on the armor of light; let us conduct ourselves becomingly as in the day, not in reveling and drunkenness, not in debauchery and licentiousness, not in quarreling and jealousy. But put on the Lord Jesus Christ, and make no provision for the flesh, to gratify its desires.

Immediately his life was changed.

Needless to say, people bring something to their life-changing situations. In Augustine's case, he had obviously been troubled by the kind of life he was leading, and, since the Bible was at hand, we can suppose he had already been reading it.

In my friend's case, she too had obviously been troubled by the thought of spending all that money on herself and her family when there were others, only a few miles from her living room, who had nothing. However, like Augustine, she was already familiar with the Bible, and she was coming weekly to church to hear it read.

So there may be two common denominators if you want your life turned around. First, you may have to feel guilty about something. Second, you may need at least a passing familiarity with the Bible. Then the Bible can deliver its wallop.

Quickly, though, it must be noted that common denominators are not conditions. There can be no conditions when it comes to the power of the Word. "The Word of God is not fettered," an early Christian wrote. Still, if the above two denominators can work in the lives of a wastrel and the woman next door, they could well be more common than we might think.

Exhilaration

There is a feeling of exhilaration that comes from preaching. Every profession has its "highs," to be sure. I was in the local hardware store today and asked the owner how he could possibly know what to do about every problem a customer brought in. "It's fun," he replied. And then he explained how each problem was a new challenge.

"I am large, I contain multitudes," Walt Whitman wrote. It is the way I feel after a good sermon. Maybe it's the preaching without notes. Maybe it's the chemistry between me and the people. Maybe it's the challenge to be interesting week after week. Maybe it's the relief when it's over. Maybe it's all of the above, but I have a hunch it's something more.

It is the power of the Word of God. I know, that sounds "mystical" and can easily be written off. But what's the matter with a little mysticism? "Christianity is not a formula for explaining everything," Albert Schweitzer once said. "The greatest knowledge is to know we are surrounded by mystery."

Both words, "mystical" and "mystery," come from the root "to shut one's mouth." I am dumb in the face of my exhilaration. I cannot describe it apart from that phrase, "the power of the Word of God." Everything else pales as description. It is the Word that ignites me. It is the Word that inspires me. It is the Word that rockets me out of bed every morning.

Remarkably, it is not just the preaching that exhilarates. It is the preparation as well. Every morning of the week, with the exception of my day off, I am alone with the Word of God. I come away feeling as if I had drunk ten cups of coffee.

Is it the poetry? Is it the history? Is it the fact that people's lives have been changed by it? Is it the fact that the world has been changed by it? Is it the fact that the world could be changed even more if more people read it? Yes. All of the above. But none of the above quite captures the meaning of the phrase, "the power of the Word of God."

Maybe the closest I can get to describing the power of the Word is to say that *my* life has been changed because of it. Every morning is fresh because of the power of the Word. And every Sunday when I open my mouth to declare the sacred mysteries, the feeling of exhilaration reaches its highest point.

Statement of Faith

It was a rare moment of revelation from one who almost never comes to church. I was surprised to hear him say it, as were the others in the group. "I stand at the window several times a day," he said, "and I look up, and I say, 'Thank you, God'."

He has had a good life. He is affluent, as Samuel Johnson put it, "beyond the wildest dreams of avarice." He has a wife and children. He has a fine job. He is a pillar of the community and was a pillar of the church.

It is this dropping out that bothers me. How could someone

who has dropped out be suddenly dropping in with such a magnificent statement of faith? My first reaction was to doubt it. The man must be a phony, I thought. If he really did thank God every day, he'd come to church. If one of his employees thought about work all the time but failed to show up, he or she would hear about it, all right, and fast.

My second reaction was to accept the statement at face value rather than judge it. After all, the only loser in the judging would be me. Why harbor the negative feeling when the positive one was so good? Even if his statement weren't true, even if he didn't stand at that window every day and say what he said he said, it was a terrific idea. All of us in the room could benefit from doing that.

I looked at the other people. They were all quiet. His simple, one-sentence sermon was obviously sinking in. Perhaps they were doing the same double-take I was. But it didn't matter. What mattered was that what he had said was working. It was having a stunning effect on all of us.

Since then, it has led me to reflect on how even my statements of faith each week can be used to inspire faith in others. They may not like me. They may think I'm a phony. They may not believe me when I say something in a sermon. But they may believe the sermon. It may have a life of its own even if the life of the messenger gets in the way of the message.

The power of the Holy Spirit is such that even the frailest vessel can be used to carry the heaviest load of truth. My friend's simple sermon to the group was as weighty a statement of faith as we were likely to hear. "I stand at the window several times a day, and I look up, and I say, 'Thank you, God'."

Chapter 7

Love in This Parish

Unconditional Love

Almost daily I pass the place where she threw herself in front of the train. She was only sixteen. I wonder whether she would have done it if she had been in our youth group.

There was a knock at my door. It was one of our senior highs. She was carrying flowers. They were for the girl's mother, she said. The girl had been her friend. But, people being who they are, the girl had never told her of her troubles.

She came, she said, because she needed strength to go to the girl's mother. She had never done anything like this before. And she had no idea how she would be received. But she was going. She felt she had to go. She wanted to go. She needed to be with her.

If only the youth group could have been there for her friend. Yes, it is idealistic, even arrogant, perhaps, to think we could have helped her. But those young people love each other. They share the ups and downs of adolescent life. They share the tears and laughter. Is it too much to suppose they could have shared her tears as well and encouraged her to laugh?

My young friend came to her church for help. When she faced the bleakest moment of her sixteen years, she came to this people, this parish. She had been coming regularly since she was eleven. We had given her the strength she sought. We had been there for her, cried with her, laughed with her, shared her troubles.

Her friend had no church. She had no place to turn, no "very present help in trouble," as the Bible says. She had no kids her own age to love her unconditionally, the same way they felt God was loving them. That was it. That was the key to what went wrong. Throughout all her failures, throughout her inability to "measure up" and "get good grades" and be "the perfect daughter," throughout, in other words, what the normal teenager goes through, there was no one, anywhere in her life, who loved her unconditionally, who mediated grace to her.

And so, without grace, there was no hope. There was no reason to go on. Indeed, there was every reason not to go on.

Church is where we are loved unconditionally. Because church is where you find people who know *they* are loved unconditionally. How do they know that? Because they know someone died for them two thousand years ago. It would be ludicrous if it weren't so pragmatic. The idea that Jesus died for them has saved a lot of people from suicide and much else. It is church youth groups that have a unique opportunity to get that idea across early in life.

We prayed. We hugged. She went on her way, smiling through her tears.

Love Place

Images of people from years ago come back to you. They are part of another people, another parish. And yet, strangely, they will not leave you. Someone's first name today triggered the image of a boy in a youth group twenty-eight years ago, even before I became a minister. What has become of him? Where has he gone? What is he doing?

I am sure it is much the same as one moves from job to job in nonchurch work. One remembers former associates. Something in the present triggers someone in the past. But there may be a difference. The minister is often involved in the deepest places of a person's life.

Take this boy, for instance. I was only a few years older. It was my first year in seminary. He would talk to me about his school, his girl, his job. I would talk about my school, my girl, my job. I began to think: how could I trace him? How could I catch up with him? Maybe he's dead.

Perhaps the difference is that in nonchurch work, the bond between people is a "performance bond." Consequently, one tends to remember—and be remembered—in proportion to one's contribution. But in a family, the bond is rarely forfeited if a performance is poor. And if the bond is forfeited because a child—or parent—does not "measure up," the consequences can be tragic. The church is more like a family than a place of work. It is a place of love, at least theoretically. The rewards of love are not based on performance. They are based on love. "It was not because you were more in number that I chose you," God says to Israel, "but because I loved you." The church says, "We love you—period." Not "We love you—if."

Churches have to be careful that they do not become workplaces rather than love places. It is easy for the church, caught as it is in the culture, to love its members *if* they perform—if they come to church, if they pledge their money, if they teach a Sunday school class. It is easy to love people if they do right. It is unconditional love that churches are asked to give because churches are representing God, who *is* unconditional love.

The leader of one of our mission projects was talking with a man who had recently been released after serving twelve years for murder. My friend found himself loving the man for who he was regardless of what he did—even when the man took a swing at my friend with a portable radio that might have killed him. He was being the church with that man. He was representing God.

Now this is not to say that plenty of people do not find their workplace to be their love place. Obviously they do. Countless people love their work, which means that they not only love what others do but love who others are. They have developed strong bonds. It only means that loving others for who they are is the church's job description. Loving others for what they do is the workplace's job description.

What I have discovered is that the mere mention of a first name can bring me the image of a former workplace, which I gradually came to know as a love place, where a boy who spoke to me then speaks to me now.

Warmth

As we were leaving church a man put his arm around a woman he had been worshiping with and said, "I love you." Their respective spouses joined them, and the four embraced. It looks maudlin in the typewriter, but it was warm in the moment. I should know. It was my wife he was embracing.

Church is moments like these. Sure, that sort of thing could happen anywhere, but it had better happen in the church or it isn't the church. Often people complain about how "cold" churches are. But all that means is that we haven't warmed them up. Nor, for that matter, has the complainer.

A woman is joining our church, and she told me how she had been looking for a year for a church that "showed love," and here at last she had found one. That may say more about her than about the church. During that year she may have learned how to embrace people.

Be that as it may, the church is in business to open up this kind of love in people. The church are the people who embrace each other. Nobody can explain it. As soon as you try to explain it, you lose it. Church people call it "Christian fellowship," but that doesn't help much. It's simply a catch-all phrase for any number of church experiences.

Perhaps the best explanation is to say that love is what Jesus was about, and churches are in business to do what he did. If you can't find the warmth the woman was looking for, then you haven't yet found a church.

A Strange History

"The Lord is with you," he said as he entered his friend's hospital room. There were tears in his eyes as he said it. Tears came to the patient's eyes as well. Both had had long bouts with illness. Both had faced death. Both belonged to the church.

It is that "belonged to the church" that is intriguing. If he hadn't belonged to a church, the first man would not have said what he did. And if he hadn't belonged to a church, the second man would not have responded as he did. "The Lord is with you" would have meant nothing to him.

But there was more to it than that. They belonged to the same church. They had a history with each other. Eventually they even found themselves in the same small group together, where weekly they had drawn strength from the fact that the Lord was with them.

How can we know the Lord is with us unless others tell us? "I see the Christ in the other," Dietrich Bonhoeffer said. "He who does not love his brother whom he has seen," the Bible says, "cannot love God whom he has not seen." The religion is in the love. The *Lord* is in the love.

Church is where we learn how to love. And we learn how because we *are* loved. Totally without merit and totally without reservation, we find ourselves being loved—by people who never knew us before. It is astounding. More to the point, it is grace. It is God. "God *is* love," we have seen the Bible say.

My two friends had never met until they found themselves in the same church. But once they found themselves there that intriguing history began. They sang the hymns and said the prayers and shared the joys and concerns of the parish together. Consequently, it was perfectly natural to see two grown men in tears in a hospital room. They were the tears of love.

Powerless

Two women are alone in the parking lot tonight. The church meeting has long since ended. As I leave, I see them talking beside one of their cars. They know that I know, although no one else knows. They are in love with the same man.

There are some things that cannot be shared. This is one. The pastor has knowledge that no one else has. At such a critical time as this, all the resources of what Paul called "God's beloved" should be brought to bear, but they cannot be, at least not now. The parties involved must work it out for themselves with the help of their God.

It is "with the help of God" that the pastor enters the picture. For weeks I have visited with one of the women, and I have talked twice with the other. But, try as I will, nothing is working. God has not been released in this process, at least not in the usual way we think of God. The usual way is for the woman who is not married to the man to bow out of the picture.

What one needs to believe in such situations is that God is present in a way that is not immediately perceived. It is like a serious illness. God must be in it somewhere; otherwise, what is the point of God? If God cares for "the birds of the air," surely God cares for us. Our problem is that we do not see God at the moment, nor even after several weeks, perhaps, or even years.

When a person comes to me, we find ourselves looking for God. We are doing everything we can to see what God wants. Some would say the will of God is clear in this instance. The pastor should tell the woman who is not married to the man, "Go and sin no more." But it is not so easy. She already knows that. She has a strong faith. The problem is she cannot help herself. That is why she has come to one who represents God. It is more than she can handle.

It reminds me of the people who come to pastors to take the so-called Fifth Step of Alcoholics Anonymous—going to a spiritual counselor to confess and repent. But the First Step is the crucial one. It is to say: "I admit I am powerless over alcohol." She has admitted she is powerless, and so we talk. But the Fifth Step escapes her. She cannot confess wrong or repent.

There is nowhere to go for help but to God. I am thrown off my own resources. So is she. We pray. But nothing seems to happen. Not yet. There appears to be no movement. God is not apparent. The night gathers around their cars. I wave to them both and leave.

The Widow and the Businessman

"I just wanted to stop in and put my arm around him and tell him I loved him." It was an older member speaking of a younger who was going through tough times. They had met in church. They wouldn't even have known each other apart from church.

Was it important that they know each other? Somehow in the divine economy it seemed to be. They were from different walks of life. She the widow; he the rising businessman. She with children who had long since grown and gone; he with children who were still there when he came home at night. She whose life had long ago been put in order; he whose life was just now falling apart. She who in her way had made her peace with God; he who railed at God for what had happened to him.

Why was it important that they know each other? Who's to say? What the church offers that most organizations do not is diversity. He has his trade association; she has her women's group. He has his Rotary Club; she has her women's club. He has his family; she has hers. He has his golf partners; she has her bridge partners. He has his dinner parties; she has hers. He has his age group; she has hers.

Now, if we could just carry out that principle of diversity around the world, the divine economy might pick up a bit. If the rich capitalists could put an arm around the poor socialists because they have the same church, even though they do not have the same politics, clearly the cause of Christ would be served. If the Catholic in Northern Ireland could do that for the Protestant and the Protestant for the Catholic, clearly it would be a victory for love. But only this week I heard of a group of people who had broken away from their church because they believed that you could not be a Christian if you did not speak in tongues. They formed a whole new church, just for the speakers in tongues.

What Jesus asked was that we love each other. "A new commandment I give you," he said, "that you love one another." There are people in the church who feel I am dead wrong in some of my opinions, or at least half-dead. We are of two minds but one heart. And that makes all the difference. Augustine said: "In essentials, unity. In nonessentials, diversity. In all things, charity." That's a good motto for a church. And when the widow puts her arm around the businessman, the motto is at work.

Wedding Ring

We had no idea it would happen that night. Our small group of eight was together. It must have seemed right to her. We were her people, her parish, her brothers and sisters in Christ. She was crying as she removed the first ring. We found ourselves reaching out. We had all left our chairs and were touching her. "This was the guard ring," she said. "And this," removing the second, "was my engagement ring." Then she removed the third.

We were hugging her. Someone kissed her finger. Each of us said something. "This is the hand that reaches out to many," someone said. And she does. She touches countless lives, but his she couldn't touch. Nor could he touch hers. It finally became necessary that they live out separately what they could not live out together. Someone began singing the Doxology. We all joined in. Then it was silent. Suddenly we found ourselves praying.

The church are the people who are with us in the depths as well as on the heights. We worship in defeat as well as in victory. God is in failure as well as in success. The trouble with "the power of positive thinking" and "possibility thinking" and "positive mental attitude" is that they tend to overlook the negative side of life. As such, they are unrealistic.

The other side of the truth that God is on the peaks is that God is in the valleys. We were in a deep valley that night in her living room. "Yea, though I walk through the valley . . . thou art with me." If God is not in the valley as well as on the peak, then where is God? Indeed, how can there be a peak without a valley? We cannot see the height without the depth.

Carlyle inveighed against Emerson's "chirpy optimism," which has nourished "positive thinkers" ever since. What such optimists tend to neglect is the power of the negative to bring the divine. When the ring is removed, God is there just as much as when the ring is put on. In this instance, with these two people, there is the candid and mature acknowledgment that they can love more apart than together and that they can be closer to Christ apart than together.

"Removing these rings," she said, "represents leaving the mainstream. Insecurity. Aloneness." But as she cried, we cried with her. In her aloneness she was not alone. Her people, her parish were with her. That's the church.

Reformatory

"Dad died this morning," he said on the phone. "Can you do the service?" You fly away to be with his family.

The autopsy showed advanced coronary disease, but there had been no hint. He called a few months ago. We had talked a year before that. I saw him once when I was back. I went over to his house. And now as I walked up the familiar drive and through the door again, it was impossible that he was not there.

Many Saturdays there would be a knock on my door at the church, and he would be there. We'd go out for coffee, and he would talk about his children, his wife, his job. Other Saturdays we would pile a bunch of teenagers into his car and take off for the state reformatory, where kids would meet kids and talk. Other days we would go to be with a man in prison whom he had taken into his home at one time. And then there would be our visits to the man who had been blown into a tree in the tornado, a man he didn't even know but had read about in the newspaper, and who was now quadriplegic.

It seemed impossible that so much goodness could suddenly be gone. As I put on my robe for the funeral, I thought of our times together and could not understand how everything could be over so quickly. I also thought how rarely he went to church. He came for a while because he wanted his children to be in confirmation, but then almost never after that. Yet he was more active than many who came regularly and gave enormously.

This does not mean that he did not miss out on a lot. Once he stopped coming he missed a whole people, a parish. He could have loved even more, had he been there for us, too. Still, he was there for all those teenagers in jail, for the man in the tree, for the ex-con in his home. He formed a new people, a new parish with each.

Being There

She had had some tough surgery. Finally she was home. An older couple from the church dropped by. "She made me soup. He brought me a McDonald's shake. I just cried. You know it— that the church is a loving community. But you don't experience it—until something like this happens."

The church are the people who are there for each other. "If one member suffers," Paul wrote, "all suffer together; if one is honored, all rejoice together." Being there is a hallmark of the church. "See how they love one another," wrote an astonished non-Christian in the third century. "See how they are willing to die for one another!"

Being there has its problems, of course. There are those who would view the milkshake and soup as intrusive. After all, elephants go off alone to die. One is reminded of the visitor to Goethe's dying mother. She sent word down that she wanted no visitors because she was "busy dying just now."

We fail at being there, too. Once in the service I shared the death of a friend. Only one person spoke of it after. I felt alone in my grief. By the same token, there are those who prefer not to share, who prefer being alone, and who have not yet experienced the joy of others being there for them. Curiously, these tend to be the same people who have trouble being there for others. They are afraid of saying the wrong thing.

There are many things one can do alone, but Christianity is not one of them. A Christian alone is a contradiction in terms. And yet there are churches to which people come to *be* alone and quiet and "get close to God." We have our share of people who leave right after the service without a word to anyone. We even have people who leave the church for good because they don't like the time in the service when we try to be there for each other. They end up in a church nearby where they can be alone and not be "embarrassed."

The couple who brought the soup and shake were there for their friend because, only months before, she had been there for them. "Bear one another's burdens," Paul said, "and so fulfill the law of Christ." That's the church.

Gypped

"He could never express his feelings." She was talking about her father, who had just died. "He'd give us things. That was his way. But I didn't want things. I wanted him. He'd never ask me to take a walk, go for a bike ride. I felt, I don't know, gypped."

Church is one of the few places where people can share their feelings. At least church at its best is. It is a mystery why more men such as her father don't share theirs. Perhaps it is our culture's emphasis on competitiveness. Perhaps it is the drive for a profit on the bottom line. Perhaps it is the baptizing of aggressive feelings in sports. Whatever it is, the American male has a hard time expressing the gentler emotions.

Church at its best is where men can do that. Unfortunately, the father in question had not experienced church at its best. "He taught Sunday school years ago," his daughter said. But that was sharing thoughts, apparently, not feelings. And if feelings had been shared at all, they were shared down, to those younger, rather than across, to his peers.

Men need a place to practice love. Church at its best is such a place. Then they can go home and show love to their families. At the end of each service we hold hands. It is a symbol of our oneness in Christ, but it is also a symbol that we are not afraid to touch each other, share our feelings for one another. Some men cannot take it. One even left the church because of it.

Jesus gathered twelve men to be a people, a parish with him. It meant that they shared feelings as well as thoughts, experiences as well as concepts. Surely the businessmen in his group were as avid for the bottom line as any today. Surely the competition between them was as keen, as we learn from the story of James and John, both wanting to be first. But as they made a church together, they built a safe harbor where they could put their emotions in dry dock and repair their inability to express themselves.

Groups of men get together here. It is amazing to see the results. I wish her father could have been among them. But we never knew him. He never came to this church. If only the one where he had taught Sunday school had had such groups. I'll bet it did. The tragedy is that such groups where men can share their feelings are available in most churches, but few men avail themselves of them.

Perhaps the pain in her life can lead to joy in other men's lives. She can elicit from them what she could not from him. As I grip the hands of the men in the pews each Sunday, I hope so.

Small Group

"I feel like a tank. I've battened down the hatches. I'm going into battle. Whenever I see any of the employees, I feel awful. One dear lady has worked there forty years. The company will not attempt to place them in new jobs." They had hired him as a consultant, and his recommendation was that nearly one hundred be fired.

The clash between economics and ethics occurs almost daily. What appears to be least ethical is often most economical. He battens down the hatches so he will not feel the pain. To be sure, short-term pain to the employee may be long-term gain to the company, but it is hard to explain that to someone being laid off.

When he shared his frustration with the other men in his church group, we were quiet. There was nothing anyone could say to relieve him of his sense of guilt. Nearly everyone in the group had been in the same position himself, either releasing people from jobs or being released. What we could do was be with him in the pain he was feeling. We told him we were, we asked the appropriate questions, and then we prayed. Someone asked for clarity so that our friend would know his recommendation was right. Another asked for peace. Another for candor. Another for love.

Doubtless there are courses in economics and ethics in business schools and management-training seminars, but what one needs at a time like this is a small group who will question one's decision and support one in the process of making and executing it. Of course, such people will not have all the relevant data, but they can ask the relevant questions. One reason he brought it up in the first place was to bounce off the rest of us whether he had done all his homework. But another reason was companionship. He needed other people with him in the loneliness of what he had to do.

When Jesus died he was alone. The cry of abandonment

came because even his closest friends had fled. That made it hard to see God. "My God, my God," he cried, "why hast thou forsaken me?" We need other people with us in our loneliness as we do what we have to do. Without them, it is hard to see God.

As we looked up from prayer, his eyes were moist. "Thanks, guys," he said.

Cardboard Scroll

I went into the pulpit one Sunday and there it was. Someone had rolled up a piece of cardboard and on it had written, "We love you." I will never know who it was. No one has claimed authorship. I don't know whether it was a child or an adult. Nor does it matter. The sentiment is all.

The pastor could just as well put a sign on the front of the pulpit saying, "I love you." In a sense, that is all the pastor does—loves the people. That is the job description. What rescues such mutuality from sentimentality is its leading to giving. If it leads nowhere, it is banal. But if it leads to the congregation's giving itself, as Jesus did, in love to the uttermost, then it is a mutuality that goes beyond the church, offering itself to the world. It is generally the most loving churches which have the most members following their money into jails, nursing homes, and slums. And it is generally the most loving churches which reach out to their own members at times of distress, such as death and divorce and job-loss and emotional crisis.

A man called to say he had been overwhelmed by the response to his hospitalization. He had gone in telling no one except me and another close friend. But word got out. A man from the church began visiting him. Another called from Philadelphia. Innumerable cards arrived. He couldn't believe it. He's not even a member of the church. Then he concluded his call to me saying, "Thanks for being in my life."

In a single instance like that, you have pastor and people in loving response to each other and to the wounds of the world. The little cardboard scroll says it all.

Hope

I am in an airplane going to a meeting in a far city. I carry you with me. You were in church Sunday, in your usual place, sitting next to your husband. You couldn't stop crying.

I would like to be able to say the right thing to take away your pain. But that is impossible. We have talked many times, and there are no words to dry your tears.

I would like to be able to say the right thing to your husband. But that, too, is impossible. I have talked with him weekly for weeks, and as he sits there stolidly beside you, I realize there is little I can do to induce him to thaw.

But you came together to worship. You are hungry for the transcendent, for something, anything, that will lift you above your pain. There is hope in that. And as I speak and you cry, the image of Naomi appears, weeping for the loss of her husband, and of her daughter-in-law Ruth beside her saying, "I will be with you." Somehow that was enough.

I will be Ruth to your Naomi. And there is hope in that.

Chapter 8

Differences in This Parish

American Flag

"I want everyone to know that if we vote for this, I will resign from the board and the church."

"If this passes," someone else said, "we might as well take down the American flag in the sanctuary." Others felt just as strongly on the opposite side. We were in a board meeting discussing whether to offer the church as a sanctuary to El Salvador refugees.

It is always a question how far churches should go in social action. Should the board risk disturbing the unity of the church? Yes, if the issue is one of Christian principle. No, if it is not. But what is Christian principle? One person's principle is another person's trifle. Unless all can agree that a principle is involved, should a board go ahead?

It is an age-old question. If Jesus had waited for the disciples to agree to go to Jerusalem, he might never have gone. If the colonists had not broken the law, which sanctuary does, by dumping the tea in Boston harbor, there might never have been an American flag. America itself is a nation of refugees. The U.N. has endorsed the political-refugee status of those fleeing El Salvador. Congress has voted to abide by such endorsements. But the State Department refuses to, so it, too, is breaking the law.

On the other hand, there are those of equally good faith who argue that such a stand on a sensitive "political" issue would divide the church because there are those who would agree with it and those who would not. You cannot say that one group is more "Christian" than the other. Besides, it is not the part of the church to be involved in such public-policy disputes. If individuals want to provide sanctuary in their own homes, that is one thing, but not the church as a corporate body with the risk of jail and fine and all that comes with breaking the law.

The two groups are at loggerheads, and the question is whether to continue toward polarization. Some would argue that that is a worthwhile risk to run. Others would argue that it is not. At the moment, we have decided to personalize the issue. Personalizing seems a good alternative to polarizing. We have had someone from outside the parish speak to us in favor of sanctuary. Now we will have someone speak against. Then we will personalize the issue even more by having refugees themselves speak to us.

Where all this will lead is anybody's guess. But what is important is the process. Good process means good product, as we have seen with regard to worship, and if people are involved in the process, and all sides are represented, then the decision that will be made will be right. At least it will be right for this people, this parish at this moment in our life together.

Having said that, however, it is important to note that something far more than the representation of "sides" is involved. We are struggling, in Paul's phrase, to "have the mind of Christ." What would Jesus do in such a situation? That is the heart of the matter. At the moment, we don't know. But with prayer, Scripture, and open, honest sharing, we believe that we will.

Bold Stroke

He came to the board meeting with a startling proposal. He wanted us to pay our benevolences first. Then if we came to the end of the year and the bills were not paid, we would either have to pay them out of salaries or go back to the congregation for more.

It was a bold stroke, and, like many bold strokes, it was too bold for some. The board immediately demurred, although their demurral was not unanimous. I was reminded of the time I suggested at a church meeting that we mortgage our church and give the money to a poor people's church. They needed it more for their building than we did for ours, I said, because our mortgage had long since been paid off. The uproar was instantaneous.

Isn't the Christian message that we put others first? "Love your neighbor as yourself," Jesus said. At the very least that is fifty-fifty. "Greater love hath no man than this," he said, "that a man lay down his life for his friends." That suggests more than fifty-fifty. He himself went all the way.

"It isn't that Christianity has been tried and found wanting," G. K. Chesterton wrote. "It is that it has been found difficult and so never really tried." As columnist George Will once observed regarding protectionism: "Free trade is just below Christianity and just above jogging on the list of things constantly praised but only sporadically practiced."

There are always those in a church who want to push faster than others. Both the pushers and the resisters feel they are bearing the Christian message. After all, it is argued, if we don't care for ourselves first we won't be able to take care of anyone else even if we wanted to. Such an assumption may be arguable, but that is just the point. It is in the argument that we will find the Christ. Somewhere in the discussion of how best to bear the Christian message, the Lord will appear.

To the pushers, that may sound like a rationalization for inaction. After all, Jesus himself was a pusher. He pushed for Palm Sunday, pushed for confrontation in the temple, pushed the religious establishment at every opportunity. But that was Jesus. He knew God's will better than either "side" in a church dispute ever will. Neither side can claim it knows the mind of Christ. Together, though, they may. Together they can bear the Christian message to the congregation at a given moment in the congregation's life. That is why votes on church boards should be unanimous. The key to the mind of Christ is in that word "together."

But doesn't that deny the prophet, the visionary, the person like the one who came to our board? Not at all. His influence will go up geometrically as he persuades the rest of the board that he is bearing the Christian message faithfully. If he can't so persuade them, then the Holy Spirit is not yet ready to move in that congregation. Better always to wait than to preempt the Holy Spirit. "Wait, I say, on the Lord."

But don't more churches die of waiting than of preemption? Because churches all across America are dying, or dead, of inertia, isn't what they need right now a host of visionaries who will have the courage to run the risk of preemption? Wasn't such courage precisely what characterized Martin Luther? And Amos and John the Baptist and Paul and Martin Luther King and Pope John and Mother Teresa?

Of course. But eventually there had to be a coalescing behind their ideas. Somewhere along the line, sooner or later, the visionary needs the pragmatist, the idealist the realist, the prophet the people. If one lone visionary at a board meeting can't get that, then it might be more prudent to fall back, wait, and organize.

It is not, incidentally, as hard as it sounds. He's got me. That's two. There were two more who liked what he said. That's four. If each gets another, that's eight. If each get's another, that's the entire church board right there. Then, if we all do this just twenty-eight more times, we will have the world. It's a mathematical fact.

Middle Ground

We have a layer of pebbles in the courtyard at the church. They remind me of the stones in the driveway of a church I used to serve. They were a symbol there. They reminded us of the money we were giving to mission which could have been used for paving the drive. Here a couple of holes were beginning to show in the already-paved drive. I suggested to the board that we not repave it but rather use the holes as a symbol of the money we could give to mission if we did not repave. They didn't go for it.

Nor perhaps should they have. I learned a valuable lesson. The values of one church cannot be transferred automatically to another. There is a curious aversion on the part of any people, any parish to hear the pastor talking about "what we did in my former church"—even though the pastor assumes that the values of one parish should be the values of another.

That is why it is always wise for the pastor to go slow when new in a church. The brouhaha with the board occurred only three years after I came. A pastor is to a church as a limb is to a tree. They grow slowly together. I was on the white pine blister rust control crew in Rocky Mountain National Park one summer. In order to eradicate the disease, we had to eradicate the carrier. We went all over the mountains, spraying the gooseberry and currant bushes with 2-4-D and 2-4-5-T. We killed them by forcing them to grow.

It can work the other way, too. The local church assumes that its values can be transferred automatically to the new pastor. Activist pastor is brought to quietist church, for example. Within months the church can be "split down the middle." Actually, the middle is where the two need to meet. It is like chess. One wins by capturing control of the middle squares. We got our $15,000 new parking lot. But a year after that we got our $100,000 mission endowment fund. Without the first, we might have had a lot of people who would not have contributed to the second. This way I learned from them and they from me. We met in the middle, and all seemed to benefit.

Social Action

It came back to me that they had decided not to join the church because they "didn't like the sermons." Translated, that meant one sermon in which I had taken a social action stand.

Differences in This Parish

It is always difficult in matters of justice to know what to do. Some will be offended when the pastor takes a stand, others will not. The evidence does not support the charge that denominational membership declines because social action stands are taken. Still, the myth persists, and in this one case the myth became reality, at least regarding two potential members.

Individual salvation is one thing, corporate another. Yet Jesus never blinked the social gospel. He did not need to ride the donkey into Jerusalem and take on the religious and political establishments. He knew such "social action" was necessary to make the point about love.

Love has two sides, the individual and corporate. The corporate side is called justice. "Love without justice is sentiment," Reinhold Niebuhr observed; "justice without love is tyranny." Both sides are needed for a full-gospel ministry. The trouble is that the one is safe, the other risky. The pastor has a choice—to play it safe or risk.

I was at a party with the offended couple recently. We stood around and talked and had a fine time. They met others there from the church. They have not worshiped with us since, but it seems to me there is hope in the social dimension of that party. The more we get to know each other, the more we can overcome our differences. "I pray for you every morning," a man said after a meeting in which we had taken opposite sides on a justice issue. "I thank God for your being here."

Clearly such love beyond disagreement is what Jesus was after when he issued his radical social demands. "Turn the other cheek." "Love your enemies." "Pray for those who persecute you." He was after a love that could withstand political differences. Going the second mile with the Roman soldier who ordered you to carry his pack was showing him that there was, at least potentially, a unity of love between the two of you that could overcome "the dividing wall of hostility," as the Bible puts it, between your society and his.

Standing around at a party and talking is hardly carrying the other person's pack, but at least it is a start.

Getting Together

There is a man with whom I have had my differences. It happens in every church. Each pastor and each member think they know what's best. Presumably they get together to resolve their differences.

We got together. Each said what was on his mind. It was open, honest. Each also said what was on his heart. It is important at times like this to share feelings as well as thoughts. At the end I said, "You're a good man."

He said, "I'd like to have more intimacy with you."

"What could we do?" I asked.

"Maybe go fishing," he replied. We shook hands, then impulsively embraced.

I have always been naive enough to think that, if both parties were willing, anything could be worked out in a church. If church is where people love each other, then love can transcend differences. This does not mean we should not differ. That would be false love. In Jeremiah's words, it would be crying "Peace! Peace! where there is no peace." What it does mean is that Jesus "breaks down" that dividing wall of hostility for the sake of "building up one another in love."

In this way the love is deepened. The differences are not minimized. They are not obliterated. They are honestly faced and openly worked through. The two parties, as in the case of my friend and me, may even agree to disagree. But that does not mean they cannot still love. Our impulsive embrace was one of the most Christian things that has happened to me of late.

So often we feel in churches that if one "side" doesn't "win" then the church will be "split" and the "losers" will leave. But that is not the way it has to be, not if people love Christ more than their differences, not if they love one another more. If we can differ strongly and still stick together, then that is a powerful love indeed. The early Christians called it "God."

Gaps

The note read, "To the finest guy I know." It was in a package left for my birthday. We had had our problems. But over the last year I had noticed a softening in our relationship. I'd drop by to see him. We'd talk. He'd buy me a Coke. We'd hold hands and pray. Each in his own way, we were bridging the distance between us. I'd throw down a pontoon with a visit. He built a Golden Gate with his present and note.

Church is curious that way. On the job, if you have problems with someone, you may work them out, but there is not always this seeming necessity to do so. But church is a place where we work at closing gaps in relationships. If we can do it there, we may be able to do it at work, home, school. Church is where we practice peace. We feel compelled to do so because Jesus "is our peace," the Bible says.

Trouble comes in churches when we forget that peace is one of our jobs. For some reason, Jesus is forgotten, and church becomes just another institution in which disagreements are allowed to fester and relational chasms are allowed to yawn. How to close gaps? one asks oneself as a church member. Such questions are necessary to creativity.

Lately another counselor and I have been working with a couple in order to close some gaps in their marital relationship. They are both members of the church. We have hit on the idea not only of working together but of meeting in my office to be sure we are in the house of God, in a worshipful setting, where we begin and end with prayer and where the four of us have a number of physical reminders of the presence of Christ. All have agreed to this creative approach to bridge-building. Whether it will work, of course, is another matter, but at least it is an attempt.

As is my friend's note. It bridged a gap. He's being creative for Christ.

135

Affirmation

We had our lunch, and it was a good time, and at the end as we said good-by in the parking lot you said, "It was a gift to be with you."

*   *   *

You called to share the excitement you felt. "It's been 115 days," you said. And then you added, "I just wanted to share it with you because I know you are with me." And we both knew what you meant—that you had been 115 days without a drink.

*   *   *

You sent me the speech you had given to your company, and it was liberally sprinkled with quotations from my "speeches" to our "company," the congregation, and you signed your letter, "Your brother in Christ."

*   *   *

I don't know of another job in which one gets more affirmation than church work. It can be deadly. Like anyone else's, the ministerial head can be easily turned. The difference is that the applause is built into this job. That is a plus, to be sure. The church is an affirming institution.

But the minus is that negative feelings toward the pastor are not always shared as easily. They go underground. And then you get the horror stories of churches in trouble because the negative feelings have finally surfaced, although too late to be dealt with positively.

That is why I counted it a gift when a woman stopped me on my way in from the parking lot last week and said, "I'm cross at you." "Why?" I asked. "Because twice last Sunday after church you turned to other people while I was talking with you and said something to them. I got the feeling you thought they were more important than I was."

"Yes," I explained, "I did. They had hurts at the moment that were greater than yours. Otherwise I wouldn't have done what I did." At the same time, however, I thanked her. So much is happening after the service that it is easy indeed to slip superficially from one person to another.

"Before," she said, "I wouldn't have said anything to you. I just would have felt self-righteous the next time I saw you. But I'm no longer invested in holding grudges." I thanked her again for that.

The unique thing about a church may be that we can share our negative feelings as affirmingly as our positive.

Anomaly

Someone said a parishioner went into my office after church to call his bookie. It was fall, with the usual Sunday football games. Apparently the service had given him an idea.

To be sure, it seems anomalous to use the pastor's phone to place a bet. But, then, we are all anomalies. It has been said that the church is not a museum for saints but a hospital for sinners. We are made in God's image, according to Genesis, and we fracture that image constantly. It is anomalous.

Time was when liquor dealers felt they could not join the church. You also hear people say they could never join a church because it would be "hypocritical." Such reasoning proceeds from a faulty premise. Church members are not perfect. They are sinners who should be biblically trying to do something about their sin. The word "sin" comes from the root for "be." Sin is being what God does not want us to be. Apparently my friend who placed the bet that Sunday came to the conclusion that gambling was not who he was. Some time later he told me he had quit.

The point of being a church is that we don't throw each

other out for certain sins. There are some churches that won't marry people who have been divorced. That's not being a church. That's being a jury. "Let him who is without sin," Jesus said, "cast the first stone." The problem is that we all fail at the bar of judgment. Who's to say that one sin is more sinful than another? Which is worse, the sin of divorce or the sin of deceit, in which a public front of unity is shown when long ago there was a private divorce? Jesus told the story of the proud man who said, "God, I thank thee that I am not like other men," and of the humble man who said, "God, be merciful to me, a sinner!"

What we need is a little more mercy in churches and a little less judgment. That way we will all be closer to the heart of the Judeo-Christian tradition, which is forgiveness. From the human point of view, such forgiveness has always seemed anomalous.

Terminating

One of the toughest things for a minister is when someone leaves the church. You can rationalize all you want. We were "on different wavelengths." "You can't win 'em all." But none of the rationalizations works.

It began last week when I was handed a three-sentence letter before church. A man and his wife were "terminating their relationship" with us. I called him for lunch. He wouldn't say why. All he would say was that he "didn't want to be a negative influence." I suggested he think of it as constructive rather than negative. He is a good man, a friend. He has served the church in many ways. But he wouldn't hear of it.

I changed my reasoning. How would he feel, I asked, if his right-hand man wrote his secretary a three-sentence letter to say he was leaving? "I'd get another one tomorrow," he said, snapping his fingers. "That's not a motivating analogy," he added. His brusqueness told me a lot about his style. If you disagree, you don't try to work it out. You leave or fire.

138

"Obviously," he said, "it is working for a lot of people. Lives are being changed. I am probably wrong. Who knows, I may be back some day." His last words as we said good-by at the door of his office building were, "I'll come by to see you."

All is never lost with God. But with humanity, this man, me, I went away sick at heart. I was up at five this morning because I couldn't sleep. Then the idea came to me, What if his son had left? That would have been a "motivating analogy," all right. Obviously he would have tried to work something out with his son—at least an understanding of why his son was leaving. But the sad fact of the matter is that, for many, the church is not as close to them as their business, let alone as close as their family. So again the analogy might have failed.

Now I am left with my feelings. He will not "come by" for weeks, probably months. He may never come by. So I will go to him again in a month or two. But I still have to live with my feelings. I try to toss it off by thinking of Jesus, who let the rich young ruler go. But it doesn't work. I can't get back to sleep.

Candor

One day I discovered why someone had left the church long ago. She didn't like the new minister. But she never told him.

Such departures happen all the time in churches. The remarkable thing is that one rarely discovers why. It is like changing doctors. No explanation is felt to be necessary. So the parishioner leaves in a fit of pique, and the pastor is left incredulous.

There are two ways of viewing such actions, we have seen. One is to say, with Jesus, "If anyone will not receive you, . . . shake off the dust from your feet." The other is to say, again with Jesus, "Go after the lost sheep." The only trouble with this second approach is that often the person has already left and is no longer receptive to a pastor's call. Consequently, it becomes necessary to take an initiative early—when there has been a drop in attendance or a sudden departure not long after the new minister arrives.

What does the minister say to the dissident member? "How have we failed you?" "How have *I* failed you?" "How have *you* failed *us*?" There is no substitute for open discussion. And it must be open. Often the church is a scapegoat. One leaves a church because "No one ever talked to me." But that can always be translated into "I never talked to anyone." One leaves a pastor, perhaps, because one never worked through one's relationship with one's parent.

The pastor's job is to keep the conversation candid. That takes courage. What the parishioner says may well apply to the church or to the pastor, and it may well be right. What the pastor says will doubtless also apply to the parishioner. But the pastor is taking the initiative for love. The pastor loves the other enough to keep them both talking until the transaction is complete, until the truth is out from each and has been named. Moses never really knew God until God revealed God's name. Then he understood the burning bush.

When a parishioner leaves a parish full of righteous indignation, it is an ideal opportunity for the bush to burn again as well as the parishioner.

Comfort

I lock the doors. It's Christmas. Everyone has gone. It is after the midnight service. The hay has been swept up from the pageant. The candles have been extinguished. The lights have been turned off.

I put my hand on the last door, the one with the reluctant lock. It reminds me of my first Christmas with this people, this parish and how I tried to lock the door and couldn't quite get it and how my friend stayed a few moments to help.

He is gone now. Not moved. Not dead. He has left the church.

I went to him. We talked. He spoke of how it wasn't the same anymore. He and his wife were no longer comfortable. It was time to move on.

I remonstrated as best I could, giving the other side to each objection. But it was no go. He had made up his mind. So had she.

A few weeks later I see them. We talk for a moment. He has the same boyish smile. She is as ebullient as ever. I hope they have rethought their decision to go. But it is wishful thinking. They are never in church again. Later I hear they have joined another.

I see them occasionally around town. He is still smiling. She is her cheery self. But tonight, as I lock the door I first locked with him, I am sad. It is Christmas. Everyone has gone. But they have gone for good.

Chapter 9

Illness in This Parish

Disparity

"They don't seem to be getting through," you say as I tell you of all the prayers coming your way from the church. And you begin to cry. The tears roll into your pillow.

"I know," I say, "it must seem impossibly hard at times."

Your daughter is combing your wig. The chemotherapy has done its work.

I think of our times together in church. I think of our dinner at the restaurant with the lighted tree. I think of our times in your home. And now you will never go home again.

Is there no way to tell you that you have an eternal home, a house not made with hands? Is there no way for the prayers to get through the pain? I want to help you die. I want to be with you in your final stage of growth.

We are there every Sunday, and we pray for you. But all the while you are here. The disparity of it must be the reason our prayers are not getting through. We are there and you are here. And we go home to our children while your children come to you here from states far away.

We send you the flowers from the sanctuary to overcome the disparity, but they only emphasize the distance between us. We send you the pastor, who goes through the sign on your door saying "Family Only" and takes your hand and reads you the Scriptures and offers a prayer. And even that doesn't work. The pain is so bad that one day you say, "I think it's time for you to go now."

Yes, we know all the stages of dying. We have read all the books. We have seen all the TV shows. We are familiar with all the admonitions to families. Your son is beside you. He takes the ice from the glass and puts it against your lips. He folds and cools the cloth and puts it across your brow. Your wall is covered with cards. Flowers are everywhere. The telephone rings.

I press the button at the traffic light, cross the street, walk down the block to my car, and drive back to the church. You are with me as I go. And you are with me now.

Failure

He was about to undergo major surgery, and he had to tell me what he could not tell his surgeon.

He had taken out a patrol in Korea, and a young man had volunteered to go with him. It was the day before Christmas and the last day of the young soldier's duty. On their way back the volunteer stepped on a mine. It blew off his leg, and he, the commanding officer, had held the boy in his arms and done everything he could to stop the bleeding while the others ran for help. The boy died in his arms with a plea to go to his mother and tell her he loved her. "I just couldn't stop it," he said. "I tried to tie off the artery, and it kept slipping out of my hands. I just couldn't stop it." The next day in surgery he might bleed to death himself.

He has carried that all this time, nearly thirty years now. Failure is not in the lexicon of a six-figure businessman, and he had failed. "I did all I could," he said. And all he could was not enough. "O shrive me, shrive me, holy man," the Ancient Mariner asked. But I could not. He is fated to tell and retell his story, and in the telling may come the forgiving.

Something has happened since his operation. He is closer to God. It is as though the telling of his story had lifted the albatross from him. He prays often. He talks openly about Jesus. He is reading the entire New Testament. He has joined one of our small groups, where we share our lows and highs. He is on his way to becoming what Paul called "transformed."

Someone else was with me as I heard his story—an elder from the church. It touched him as deeply as me. He said that our being there with our friend at that particular time was more important than any business that he could remember having transacted on the church board. This *was* the official business of the board. "If only," he said, "we could have our board meetings at hospital bedsides, it would change the entire character of the church."

"Is any among you sick?" wrote the author of James. "Let him call for the elders of the church." If any people need to experience the new creation, it is the official boards of the church. Because then, from them, emanates the new creation into the life of the congregation. Little did the former marine know that in his confession of failure were the seeds of success for his church. "The blood of the martyrs," ran an early Christian saying, "is the seed of the church." In the death of a boy at Christmas a man was reborn and a church was brought to new life.

Magnolia

"Tell me everything," he said. "Don't hold anything back." So they didn't. They told him it was bone cancer. They said he had a year to live. He called his wife, told her the news, and said, "Come up for dinner. We'll have a date." She came to his hospital room, and they talked and laughed and ate together. And prayed.

It was not false courage. Nor was it repression. He is in his seventies. He has lived a good life. He will continue to enjoy life until he dies. He bent every effort to leave the hospital while their star magnolia was in bloom. He made it.

Every morning begins with the Bible and prayer. No, it is not something he has hit upon since his illness. He's done it for years. "I hope everyone prays for me," he said. It was as natural as leaves to his tree. He's that kind of guy.

You wonder where it came from, this acceptance of death as

part of life. Maybe it is a function of age and "we all have to die some time." Maybe it is how he was born. He may be a natural for accepting life's tragedies. But who is, really? Maybe it is how he was schooled. He was imbued with the "stiff upper lip." Maybe he has had shock after shock in his life, and this is just one more for one who is already inured.

On the other hand, maybe it's God. Maybe God *is* what enables us to accept death. And maybe God works for him because he had allowed God already to enable him to accept life. After all, how many people who played football against the Four Horsemen of Notre Dame want to get home to their star magnolias as they lie dying and ask their wives to their hospital rooms for a date?

You

You, going brittle while the iron lung sighs you alive. You, painting with your teeth while you watch the world on your back through a mirror. You, raising money for charity and having celebrities visit. You laugh and say, "Praise God. The credit belongs to him." I'll buy that.

Doubt

I looked up after praying, and there was a tear on each of her cheeks. She believed, and she didn't. She is committed, but she also doubts. And it is times like these that bring the doubts. She has been sick for months.

We have thirty people who pray for those in distress. In

addition, a call to pray is issued weekly to all in the church. But none of it seems to have worked. She is as sick as when we started to pray. Indeed, she is worse, and the doctor is not at all optimistic.

It is a test for others as well as for her. The comments keep coming back. "What's taking so long?" "Why isn't she better?" "Where's God in all this?"

One way out is to say it is in God's hands and leave it at that. But that is fatalism. "Que sera sera," whatever will be will be. Surely we can do something. "Whatever you ask in prayer," Jesus said, "believe that you receive it and you will." We believe that, but we don't see it happening. So we doubt it, too.

One tear for faith, one for doubt? Our honesty is all we have to bring to God. "I believe," the man with the sick daughter said to Jesus, "help my unbelief." Then she was healed.

Serene

She fell on the basement stairs. It took her an hour to get to the phone. She had broken her hip and her wrist. It is now two weeks and two operations later. Her husband calls to thank the church. "She will be fine," he says.

It is hard to believe such resilience. There are no complaints when I see her. She is in pain, but it does not erase her smile. She was twelve hours in the emergency room, much of it waiting for attention. Then they set the wrist wrong, and it had to be broken again. She laughs as she tells me.

It was three years ago that she called. We would get together from time to time. Out of one of those times came the idea of a prayer group. She has been meeting with a dozen or so women every week since. It is impossible to say how many lives she has touched. She has her anxieties, which she shares with the others, but she is also, if you can believe such a paradox, serene.

Some day I will ask her to what she attributes her tranquility. But she will not be able to tell me. It is the nature of faith that it cannot explain itself. It is like the mercury from the broken thermometer on the bathroom floor. You can't pick it up.

Nor is it necessary. What we have in the hospital bed is someone at peace. The nurses sense it. Small wonder that when I arrived one day she was insisting they take some of her flowers. Small wonder that she had so many flowers in the first place. When the nurses know that the spirit is healing the body, you can sense it. There is a lift to the hospital air.

So good night, good lady. You are fine, all right.

Gift

It was a very large gift. They wanted it to go toward helping a man visit his wife in a hospital far away. She would be there a long time. Her illness was difficult. They wanted the gift to help others from the church see her, too. It was not only that she meant that much to us. We meant that much to her. She needed us emotionally as much as she needed her doctors physically.

There is no end to the care shown in a church. Events like this are duplicated every day in churches everywhere. It's as though being a church together brings out the best in people. People want to do things like this. Their imaginations are kindled, then their volitions. Thought becomes act; intention, event.

They wanted it to be anonymous, which was most imaginative indeed. "There is no end to the good you can do," it is said, "if you don't care who gets the credit." The purpose of the gift to this couple was not credit. Regarding the gift, the letter to the church said that "the purpose is to share their burden and that they might feel loved." As Paul wrote to the early church, "Bear one another's burdens."

A number of weeks later she came home to a hospital here.

People from the church were with her daily. We prayed with her. We anointed her with oil, as the Epistle of James suggests. Remarkably, she began to improve. One day her doctor made a beeline for me from the nurses' station. "Tell the people at church," he said, "to give us doctors at least some of the credit." Soon she was released. To this day she says she was healed not only by her doctors but by her God.

One aspect of her healing was this people, this parish. With all the animals and balloons people brought her, her room was a cross between a zoo and a circus. Regularly it was turned into a convention center. And always, it was a church. Two or three were constantly gathered in Christ's name, first in the hospital far away and then in the one closer to home.

A letter came a few days after her release. "We feel very blessed," her husband wrote. "Please use this for someone who may need it more." Enclosed was a check for the same amount as the gift. Once the gift of love has been given, it goes on giving. It has a momentum of its own.

Coma

"Are you his father?" the nurse asked as I looked down on his prostrate form. He stared blankly ahead, seeing no one, hearing nothing. He had been in a coma for months, and the doctors had said there was no hope. But every day someone was there from the church praying beside him. Would he ever wake up?

His parents came from another state to be with him as long as they could. His wife, who had just had their third child, was with him each day. His children came. They were just old enough to realize what was happening, and it scared them.

Every week in church we would pray. People would come up to his wife after worship. Food was brought into the home.

Babysitters appeared. Her parents were there day and night. What if it had been my son? Could I have dealt with it as well as they did?

The church are the people who pray for each other. "Pray for one another," wrote James to first-century Christians, "that you may be healed." So often prayer is the last resort when it should be the first. Often we need a crisis to bring us to our knees.

The mystery of faith is that people often do not come to Christ until they have been through an upheaval. An even greater mystery is that it is possible to come close to Christ through someone else's upheaval. Her reports to the congregation on her husband's progress and regress were remarkable. She was soft-spoken, radiant. She was being used to communicate a faith that is stronger than death. Just as Jesus' vicarious suffering opened the way for believers to approach a holy God, so also the suffering of another can be the means God uses to draw us closer to himself.

If it were my son, as it once was God's son, I would hope that I, too, could be used to brighten lives with that same faith. As the pastor of Augustine's mother said of him as she wept and prayed, at the lowest point in Augustine's life, long before he became a Christian, "It is impossible that the child of such prayers and tears should perish."

When she told us he woke up, the whole congregation burst into applause.

Tough Love

He called early one morning. "It's me," he said, and he gave his name. "Could you come over? I've been drinking again." I took a deep breath and said, "No." I had come on several occasions before, I explained, and now it was time for him to call AA. "I can't do that," he said, and hung up.

It is now four days later, and I am still bothered by my "tough love." Long before, I had steeled myself to do it, but when the time actually came it was hard not to go. As a pastor I instinctively go when one of this people, this parish hurts. I am reminded again of the fact that Jesus taught that the normal caring shepherd would leave the ninety-nine safe sheep and search for the one that was lost.

Twice we have gotten him to hospitals. Twice he has walked out after three to five days, long before the twenty-one-day program was over. His own doctor was in AA himself and has been trying for months to get him to go. He told us he goes from one set of friends to another for rescue.

When I reached his house last night, there were three newspapers on his doorstep. I rang the bell and looked in. I imagined the worst and hoped for the best. I hoped it had worked out for him but was not at all sure that it had. Now I am alone; and even though a recovering alcoholic has helped to reinforce my decision, I still hurt for my friend and the No that I gave him.

There is another side, of course, to what Jesus did. He told the rich young ruler to sell what he had and give to the poor, and that rich man "turned away sorrowing." "I come," Jesus said, "not to bring peace but a sword." What is difficult is knowing when to be tough and when to be tender. All I know at this point is that now, in the early morning of the fourth day after he called, I agonize for my friend.

I picked up his papers and left.

Intensive Care

I go back and forth between the intensive-care rooms. We have one person in one and another across the way. Neither is expected to make it. The nurses come and go. It is quiet but busy. I take her hand. Tubes are everywhere. She does not know me. She does not know anyone. She cannot even squeeze my hand. I pray violently.

Across the way I take his hand. His vital signs are better, but still there is no recognition. He is awake but sees no one. I bend close to his ear. There is no sign. Nothing.

Some would call it a fruitless exercise. Others would call it absurd. The doctors allow it. The nurses bear it. Neither remark it. They appear to be neutral. Or embarrassed. They just don't want to deal with it. Prayer is my job, not theirs. Every little bit helps. That sort of thing.

But maybe something communicates to them as well as to the patient. Maybe they realize that there is an alliance of body and soul, that what happens to the one profoundly affects the other. It has been estimated that sixty percent of all visits to doctors are for psychosomatic symptoms. The doctor deals with the *soma,* the body, the pastor with the *psyche,* the soul. Thus doctor and pastor could forge an alliance. But they never do. I have never been called by a doctor about a patient. I have called doctors myself, but it never goes beyond "show him support." "Help her family understand." That's pretty pale stuff.

I greet my friend in the hall. "Hi, Preach," he says. She is his patient. He knows he is losing her. He told her before the operation that it was "iffy." Her body is just worn out. The trauma is too much. But what about her soul? That's the pastor's department. Only prayer can save her now, people say.

At the funeral the familiar words are read, the things about her said. We take her to a hilltop, then go to her home for coffee and cake. The body is under, the soul above. The alliance is broken again. *Psyche* and *soma* are split. But are they? "I believe in the resurrection of the body," we said in the Apostles' Creed at her service. In death *psyche* and *soma* would unite, even though in life they appeared to be split, at least medically. If they can be joined in death, think what could happen if pastor and doctor worked to join them in life. Joined, they are what the earliest Christians called "the new creation," the one in which body and soul are united by Christ.

The man across the way? He was in church Sunday.

Nursing Home

"Happy Springtime!

I'm not sure of the name of the person to whom this should be directed, so I'll just send it to you folks in the office to pass it on to the proper authority. In the past, when I was employed, I had been trying to tithe; I'm still trying. I am allowed $25.00 each month from my Social Security check—the rest is taken by the nursing home here. $2.50 seems like such a very small amount, but I guess a little is better than nothing. Just returning a small portion of the blessings the Lord has so generously bestowed on me and my loved ones.

Thank you, and bless you. Until next month—"

Next month:

"Dear Friends,

Enclosed is my June offering of $2.50. I have added $3.00, which is 10% of what I earned from the sale of one of my paintings.

Praise the Lord!"

Next month she was dead.

Squint

"I just wanted you to know they're operating on Bill this morning. He began to lose his peripheral vision. They say it could be either a tumor or blood clot. I just thought you might remember him in your prayers."

They were in the family room when I arrived. The news had

154

just come down. It was a clot, not a tumor, and it had been removed. He said, "I can see." Apparently it was a total success. People were using words such as "miracle," "prayer," and "God." The doctors were using phrases like "hole as big as a coffee cup."

She had called me. The pastor represents the presence of Christ at moments like these. Indeed, each of us in a church represents Christ to the other. And each tries to "see" Christ in the other. A note on our refrigerator reads: "If you can't see the Christ in someone, squint." It's a good reminder of what our job is. At the bottom it says, "Women's Retreat." They knew that there was no church apart from each other.

There is only one way to bring Jesus out of nowhere into now, here. It is through one another. We would not even know Jesus if it were not for someone who had told us. Even an experience like Paul's, in which no other Christian was present at first, was prefaced by hearing about Christ from the very Christians he was arresting.

As the news came down from Recovery, we embraced, forming a church within the church, two or three gathered in his name.

Your Last Picture

I found you in your garret studio surrounded by your watercolors and your bed. You were a sometime painter and sometime church member. How glad you were to see me. You were old now and couldn't get out much. So we brought the church to you, and you were content.

One day they moved you to the county home. I found you there long after. Your bed was the fourth one on the right. Across from you twelve others lay. All your life was in a little bag you could not reach beside you on the floor. It reminded me of those pictures in the books of the young man leaving home with a stick over his shoulder and the same little bag tied on.

This was to be your last journey. We both knew that. But still you greeted me with the same enthusiasm as before. It made me think of the Greek I had learned in seminary not long before and how the word "enthusiasm" comes from the Greek for "God within." You had a measure of God I had not found before. "Good measure," Jesus said, "pressed down, shaken together, running over." Yes, you had that.

The long room smelled of feces, urine, and decaying flesh. It would not have been a pretty picture for you to paint. And yet, in your way, you were painting the most stunning picture I had seen. I had stood before the Mona Lisa in the Louvre, the Night Watch in the Rijksmuseum, and the View of Toledo in the Met, but the picture you painted, with the last of your watercolors on the floor beside your bed, left me breathless. You never complained. You never cried. You always smiled. You asked about me, about my family and the church. You talked about God. We prayed.

And then I went away from you, as pastors often do, to another parish in another state, and one day word came back that you had reached your destination on your final journey. You had painted your last picture, and I had not been there to see it. And yet, strangely, I carry it with me. It is a picture of you, in the fourth bed on the right, with your rapid smile and your talk to the youthful pastor about God. Your picture has been with me in all the garrets and the county homes where I have found myself, since first I climbed the ancient stairs to your watercolors and your bed.

Chapter 10

Death in This Parish

Dying

As you lie there, you barely speak. I lean forward to catch a word, a phrase. You are planning your funeral. "Make it short," you say. "Nothing drippy." And then you ask for your favorite hymns.

The cards along the window sill are brave but few this time. The phone calls have long since stopped. Only your husband and family see you now. And, at this moment, we are alone.

You take my hand. I bring you greetings from a friend. You smile. I read some verses, pray. Our hands are tight. As I bend to say Good-by, you draw my head to yours and kiss me on the lips.

A Great Run

His AA group sent him a card as he lay dying. They had all signed. It was a huge card and it stood in the window beside his bed. He had been with them every week for ten years, and they sent him a card.

I often wonder why we are so timid about death. If we are Christians, we believe that death is not the last word, God is. We come together at funerals to celebrate a life even more than to mourn a death. And not just the life lived but the life beyond life. "I am the resurrection and the life. He that believeth in me, though he were dead, yet shall he live."

But only four or five of them came. The rest left him to do his own dying. I cannot believe it was because they "respected his privacy." Christianity is not private. AA itself was started by a minister and a parishioner. When a person calls AA, another AA is there within minutes. One never meets in AA alone. There is no such thing as an AA meeting with only one person present. If we need others to help us with our drinking, surely we need others to help us with our dying.

Maybe they stayed away because the family told them to. Families will do that, although this one didn't. But why should the loving circle narrow at death rather than expand? Clearly people he had been close to for ten years were part of his larger family. And any one of them, with only a modest degree of assertiveness, could have come for a moment or two.

Maybe it was because they were afraid to confront their own dying. "I can't stand hospitals," we say. It is because we are afraid of the intimations of mortality they give. If one that close were dying, one of them could be next. It upset the dynamic of the group. Better to deny, as in the first years of alcohol, than to deal. An ironic reversion.

"It's been a great run," the minister cofounder of AA wrote his friends as he lay dying. It had been a great run for my friend, too. What a life he had lived. And as I bent over his bed to give him his last communion, the card from his friends caught my eye. It was their way of saying, the best they could, that it had, indeed, been a great run.

Stranger

You get the call from the funeral home. You will do what you can, of course. But you have never met the family before. They belong to no church. It is his father who died. Retired. Florida.

You meet the funeral director at the door. You go into the chapel and meet the family. The service was in Florida. This is the interment ceremony. He will be put in the wall down the way from the chapel. We are in a "memorial garden."

You do your job. You read the Scriptures, offer the prayers, say a few words. You hope you hit the mark. You look twice to be sure of his name.

When it is over they are effusive. There has been a connection. You wonder how it happened. You are unknown to them. They stumble over your name. They live two suburbs away. You will never see them again. But you have been together. And for that brief moment it was good. Perhaps this is all we have anywhere with anyone. Moments. And in the moments, God.

Half-Life

He came back to church after his divorce. The church made him a deacon. He also taught Sunday school. Then he was gone. He had moved away, we discovered. I would call occasionally, but there was never an answer. When he went to the hospital, no one knew. When he left the hospital, he went to his son's. One day his son's wife called. He had died.

"He was private," his son explains. "Even if you had taken him out to lunch, he would have shown you only a small part of himself. He was skilled at turning the conversation away from himself and onto you. He only told you half of what he felt. Not even his sons knew him." And now he is gone, taking the other half with him.

We only have what we gave when we die. It is good to go to the grave empty. He gave a lot. But he had so much more to give. "Life should go down foaming in full body over the precipice," Robert Louis Stevenson said. He should have known. He was dying of tuberculosis.

How do you explain anonymous dying to this people, this

parish? That we are not a people, not a parish, when we don't even know that one of us is dying, one who has been at the very heart of our life together, teaching the little children, calling on the sick? Could it be that all our talk about being, or at least trying to be, the "beloved community" that Paul describes is in vain?

The answer lies in what Paul called "participation" or *koinonia*. My friend had no feeling that he was a participant any more. He felt he no longer belonged to the church family. When he came back we were different. Many of his old friends had moved on. He didn't know us. Maybe that is why he related to children but not to the rest of us, except as he would be assigned a call as a deacon. Come to think of it, he did not make many of those calls. He was always too busy.

I was surprised to see two from the church at the funeral home as I walked into the chapel. How encouraging it would be to him to know that we were with him in death if not in life. But he was gone, his casket half-open behind me, his life half-given. And our life only half-given, too. Only three of us there at the end out of six hundred. "He was private," his son said. But so were we.

Terminal

I walk into your room and talk to you. Your eyes are half-open. I say the Shepherd's Psalm you love, and there is nothing, not even a flicker. I pray, and it trails off. The i.v. keeps draining, and there is nothing.

I pick up my coat from the chair, nod to the woman in the bed nearby, leave my mask in the bag by the door, walk slowly down the hall, and now am on the stairs saying, "God."

Smile

I'd come to your room and you'd smile and we'd talk. When I left, you would give me a handshake that reminded me of the machines you sold. You were as strong inside as out. I'd go away shaking my head in disbelief.

It was not that you were denying your cancer. As a former medical man in the service you knew what was happening. You just wouldn't let it get the better of you. We all know of cancer patients who rode it out with grim courage. You were different. There was no irony in your smile, no stiff upper lip to mask what was happening below, no grimness. Even when your appliance broke and they rushed you, bleeding, to the hospital, there you were in emergency taking my hand and welcoming me with your smile.

People sensed the difference. After the funeral, we were all at your house. No one was moping. We were enjoying the cold cuts as we talked about you. Your wife introduced me to all who had come, some from great distances, to be with you. It was a substantial number.

How to explain it? One can reflect, perhaps, and not need to explain. What we were doing at your home after the service was reflecting on your life. You didn't speak much these last months, and when you did there was no macabre humor, no self-pity. It was just something that had happened to you and you'd get on with it, much as you had with everything else in life, like the selling of your automotive machines, which took you away from your family so much.

I don't think you even went through Elizabeth Kübler-Ross's five stages of dying—denial, anger, bargaining, despair, and acceptance. I doubt that you had ever heard of them. And if you had, I doubt that they would have meant much. They were too analytical. Your illness just was, and you'd handle it as best you could. The best analogy might be to George Leigh-Mallory, the pioneer of Mount Everest, who, when asked why he wanted to climb it replied, "Because it is there."

We didn't discuss religion much. There was no need. You had ushered at the church for years. You were there every Sunday. Jesus was real to you. Being with you reminded me of what Paul had said while he awaited death: "I can do all things in him who strengthens me."

You went out tough, my friend, quiet, smiling. Over the cold cuts everyone knew it. They knew the power of Christ in your life. They knew it *had* to be Christ. Thanks for the witness. You've been another Paul for us.

Follow-Through

His mother died and I went over and we prayed. She lived in another city. He would fly out the next day. We held hands around the table. The smallest child did not understand. She squirmed on her mother's lap. The older children had left the TV on in the other room. We embraced each other as I left.

I'll see them at church and we'll be together at parties and meetings, but we are not likely to be together again about his mother. And yet she has died. He grew up with her. He went off to college. He got a job, married, had a family. She was in on all that, and now she is dead, and all we could do was bow our heads about it and hug.

Yes, that's something. Some would say it's a lot. I'm not so sure. Your mother dies and the pastor comes over and you get on an airplane and that's about it from this people, this parish. There will be cards, phone calls, meals, or course, and that will wrap it up. But your mother is dead.

Follow-through is what separates perfunctory churches from serious ones. Will this people, this parish be going back? Will this pastor? The only way I have been able to do that is to put such people into my datebook a week, a month, three, six, and twelve months hence, and then every year after. It seems like a travesty of church to have to put a church member into your datebook, but I know of no other way to do it. The remarkable thing is that so many of the people in the church do the same. After all, the pastor is supposed to. That's the pastor's job. But when others do it, then you have a serious church.

A serious church doesn't forget the sons of mothers who have died. The calls and visits keep coming. The hugs.

Funeral Home

I am sitting in a funeral home waiting to be called for the service. The memories come of other funerals in other funeral homes. I hear the same quavering organ. I smell the same flowers. I see the same worshipers ghosting in. Every sound is swallowed by the acoustical ceiling-tiles. The funeral directors are in their funereal suits. Around the corner lies a body in an open casket, the next service after ours.

The purpose of a funeral is to bring the dead person to life. I have been to the family's home a day or two before and taken down from them what made this child of God unique. I add their thoughts to mine. We are bringing that uniqueness as our offering in the service. There will be tears, but there will also be smiles. Anything goes to make the person live for those who have come to celebrate his or her life.

A funeral's purpose is also to bring Jesus to life. Attention is to be so riveted to him that there can be hope beyond death. Consequently, anything goes to make Jesus live for those who are there, many of whom have no people, no parish, particularly if the service is in a funeral home. It is no easy task. Eyes glaze. Heads nod. Faces freeze.

Much of the problem, aside from the pastor's not being up to the task, is the funeral home itself. The carpet is heavy, the flowers oppressive, the chairs in a row, the lighting dim, the lectern frail. Most funeral directors I know would be happy to have the service in the church, but somewhere along the line people began to associate funerals with funeral homes. It drains the life from the service.

As I reflect on all the funerals I have done in such places, I realize something must be done. First, I will educate the parish in sermons to come back to church. Second, when the next call comes from a funeral home to have the service there, I will ask the director to ask the family to have the service where it belongs. Third, if the above two fail, the next time we have a service in a funeral home, it will be one that will melt the glue on the acoustical tiles.

Communion of Saints

The hardest thing is the people you leave behind. It is never easy for a pastor to change churches. The people from the former parish are always with you. And when I heard a short time back that one of my good friends from a former parish had died, I was sad.

You want to be there and you are, of course, a thousand miles away, and it is completely impractical. So you settle for a phone call or letter. Within the past three months I have written one letter and made one call.

Then there is always the thought that you could have been closer to your parishioners when you were there. You realize that such a thought is natural in any grief, but it does not help.

Then come the resolutions to be closer to the people you are with at this moment in your life. But often such thoughts trail off after a week or so.

One way to handle a friend's death is to look on the past without guilt and the future without fear. That is a tall order, to be sure. It adds up to making the most of the moment. Maybe the church are the people who help keep us in the present. And when one of them dies, we need the others to keep us present to Christ.

Last night a woman shared in a group that one of her closest friends had died. Spontaneously, others responded from their own griefs and, haltingly, from what they thought the Word of God might be saying to her and to them. Wherever the church is, in death or life, it is now. Surely that is what is meant by the communion of saints.

Meaning

Tonight I reflect on four of us who may be dying. It is tearing the heart of this people, this parish. Where is the justice in a brilliant executive's dying before his time? In a young woman's grave illness? In a man's making great strides in putting his life back together only to have it taken away? In another man's looking forward to a retirement which may never come?

There *is* no justice in such deaths. No theodicy can be manufactured to fit. Indeed, one could argue that premature death is so unjust that if a loving God allows it, then that kind of God is not loving. This is the commonest argument against the existence of God: if there were a God, evil would not be permitted.

Nor is there any sense in such deaths. Of course, I cannot understand them. No one can. To try to do so is futile. Everyone knows that. Job railed at the injustice of his children's deaths, tried to understand it, found that he could not, and gave up saying, "I have uttered what I did not understand."

Most Christians find that the best exit from such a dilemma is to say that, although premature death is unjust and nonsensical, it is so only in a proximate, not in an ultimate, sense. Ultimately, life is meaningful, even if it ends too soon. Proof is the premature death of Jesus. Proximately, it made no sense. Ultimately, it makes more sense than any other event in the history of the world.

To many, such an assertion of ultimate meaning beyond proximate meaninglessness is the ultimate in absurdity and injustice. It is an article of faith to which only the credulous subscribe. "Rational" people do not make such subscriptions. They are neither so gullible nor so naive.

Perhaps. But rational Christians, such as these four, see powerful evidence for ultimate meaning, if not for ultimate justice. The best evidence for the Resurrection, it has been argued, is the existence of the church. One does not go to the gallows for a myth. One does not allow oneself to be burned as a lamp at one of Nero's banquets for a dream. One's life is not changed for a fantasy. The hypothesis of ultimate meaning proved such a workable one that a third of the world is now Christian.

No, that does not prove the hypothesis. It does not establish the objective reality of God. It does not confirm ultimate meaning. Nothing can. Hence faith. Faith by definition is hypothetical. But the hypothesis is chosen, in what Kierkegaard called the Christian's "leap of faith," because the hypothesis works. My four friends are doing their dying with a calm that is remarkable. More to the point, their calm is itself evidence for the ultimate meaning of life, even if not for the ultimate justice of premature death.

Death of a Young Mother

It must have happened as I bent over fruitcake at the dinner party. I passed the ambulance going the other way on the four-lane highway with its light revolving, no siren, through the night. I thought nothing of it until the call came.

Her husband was there, smiling, and we were with him—

two, three, four hours. Finally the doctor came out. "There is no hope," he said. "It is just a matter of time. The impact was such that when the other car hit hers . . . ."

Her husband picked up the paper bag of her things—her purse, her dress, her shoes. And after we had stood some more under the long fluorescence we left—the attorney, the neighbor, the brother, the sister-in-law, and I.

Her mother came and joined the vigil. The whole church prayed around the clock. "It's coming close, Mom," he said. She tugged the jewel around her neck the way her daughter had.

"Take care on the road," her husband said to me one night. "Can I get you a cup of coffee?" He took my two hands. "This is our faith," he said. I went to my car and wept.

She was my right arm, my colleague. We did everything in the church together. She had been president of the student body in her sophomore year in college. She had four beautiful children. I loved her. Everyone did.

He waited outside our house until the lights went on, then knocked softly and called to my window to tell me the end had come. "How are you doing?" he asked.

She died just down the hall from where her third child had been born, while her killer sobered up on orange juice in the bed across.

Great Expectations

Your car drew up, and I left your family to meet you at the curb. You had been away on a business trip, and, driving home, they had been unable to reach you. "John," I said, as you got out of your car, "your father died this morning." It had not been expected.

It put me in mind of another home I had been to with similar news. How the marine officer and I approached the door and

168

rang and how, when she saw us, the young man's mother clutched at her throat and said, "Oh, no." Fortunately, it wasn't that bad. He had only been wounded. Later, when he came home, he went on a hunting trip and died at an icy bend in the road.

The pastor is there when the unknown and unexpected meet. Suddenly there is a turn in the road, and we are off the highway of life. The pastor arrives to bring divine truth, to bear the message that something is known of the unknown and that we do know something of what to expect beyond death.

The pastor is there as an emissary of the church, the people of God, the people of transcendent knowledge and transcendent expectation. No, we do not know everything. Nor do we ever know enough. We are always eager to know more. But the Bible goes only so far. The funeral service itself can reach into the unknown only so far.

My father died of leukemia just two days after his eightieth birthday. His death had been expected for two years. It gave him time to mediate the transcendent to us. I remember calling one day to see how things were going. "Don't worry about us here," was the cheery reply. "The goose hangs high."

It was not denial. It was not bravado. It was Christian nonchalance in the face of death. He knew something of the unknown, not everything, to be sure, but something, and enough, just enough, for the goose to hang high. He also knew what to expect—not exactly, but enough. He ended his conversation with me by quoting John Buchan:

> Far from the heather hills,
> Far from the misty sea,
> Little it recks where a man may fall,
> If he falls with his heart on Thee.

At his funeral the worshipers were invited to say what he had meant to them. Each comment was a revelation of the unknown; the memories of courage, wisdom, and love reminded us of how his life had always been attached to what would endure beyond it. We buried him next to his parents in front of the big rock, and as each grandchild put a shovelful of dirt on his grave, the hermit thrushes sang, deep in the woods, reminding us that what lay beyond us would more than meet our expectations and would be beautiful beyond the telling of it.

We reached out to one another in your living room and prayed fervently. It reminded us of what we knew in what we didn't know and what we could expect when the unexpected came.

Rite of Passage

It was the day before Palm Sunday, and just as the waiting time for Holy Week was almost up, so his time was almost up. He reached over to a folder that obviously contained his most precious papers. He showed me a picture of his family, and then he found what he was looking for. It was a letter from one of the men in the church. He had saved it for more than a year. He told me to read it.

It was a letter of encouragement from one who had been discouraged about his own health, too. But what was extraordinary about it was that it abounded in hope and joy. He had ended it with a quotation from the Bible: "May the God of hope fill you with all joy and peace in believing, so that by the power of the Holy Spirit you may abound in hope."

"Here," my friend in the hospital bed said, "take it to Jim." He wanted the letter writer to have his letter back—so that it would, in turn, sustain him when his health went bad again. It was a simple gesture, and somehow a rite of passage.

He was passing on the faith which had been passed to him. He was giving it back so it could continue to be given. He knew that the letter writer would write again, to countless other people, and this was the dying man's simple way of saying, "Thanks for writing me. God bless you for passing on the faith."

Always!

She typed it out and put it in her will. I was so moved on hearing of it that I asked her for a copy. She was reluctant to share it. After all, it was between her and her children. So I said that, of course, I understood, and withdrew my request. Two weeks later it came in the mail.

She was willing her faith to her children. I had never seen anything like it. Nor have I since. We put all our goods and chattels in our wills, all our prized possessions, but our most prized?

> I pray because I believe prayers are answered.
> I am able to believe prayers are answered because
> mine have been. I believe in God and His love
> for us. He is real. In prayer I try to surrender
> my own will, as I can see only a little way.
> When I pray, I am asking where I should fit into
> this day. Prayer puts the pieces together for
> me—not instantly, but usually from it a bit of
> insight follows which guides me.

It goes on in this vein for three single-spaced pages. Finally, toward the end she wrote:

> I am grateful that I can totally believe in a
> life of some kind beyond this because of
> Christ. God's love is too great to have
> created man for just an instant. God is here,
> with you, always!
>
> Love,
> Mom

God is here, with us, always! This people, this parish remind me of that.

Aging

I remember how you had been away, and now you were back, waiting for me after the service. You had been called out of town for "illness in the family." But I could tell by your eyes that it had been more than just illness. You told me that your sister in the far city had died.

Your tiny body, which is always so straight, was slumped this morning, and the fire in your eyes burned low. Perhaps you were thinking how sudden it had been, and how you had had so little time to be there. Perhaps you were thinking of your own death, and how it is there each night to haunt you because you are old, too. Perhaps you were glad to be back with your sisters and brothers in Christ, and it may be that your being back is what enabled the fire to burn as high as it did and your back to be as straight as it was.

We hugged, you remember, and kissed, and then you were gone, a pheasant among the corn. May the hunter never find you. But when he does, we will have such a celebration as this church has never seen. We will celebrate your life, and we will celebrate your life beyond life. Because you have been at the heart of this people, this parish for years. And by your immense caring and acute mind you have given more people a glimpse of Jesus than you will ever know.

Chapter 11

The Pastor in This Parish

Fountain

I come back from taking my friend communion. It is the first Sunday in Lent. I sit by the memorial fountain with my head in my hands, listening to the water. My friend has cancer. He knows it will not be long. His outlook is as bright as ever, but he knows. The poinsettias from Christmas are still blooming. I plunge my face into the fountain. I want to be clean, clean.

Sometimes it is too much. I yearn for someone to call me and say he or she knows it is too much. His illness is known throughout the parish. So is that of the others who are ill and divorcing and losing their jobs. But no one calls, and plunging my face in the water is as if to relieve me of the pain of this people, this parish.

The pastor has a spouse, of course, and failing that, or in addition, one or two trusted friends. But the loneliness of pastors is not usually known. Indeed, the opposite is assumed. When one is the spiritual leader of anywhere from a few hundred to a few thousand people, it is assumed that one will be called, not once but several times.

All that is needed is someone to say, "I know there's a lot of heartache in the parish right now, and I just wanted to tell you I'm thinking of you." If only one person were to do that, he or she would be remembered for life. Pastors never forget parishioners who take such initiatives with them. Occasionally parishioners do. I need someone to now.

As much as anything, the cult of the expert is to blame. Experts are supposed to have the answers, not need them. At the very least, an expert does not need his or her hand held while searching for answers. And when it comes to such ultimate questions as death, it is objected that there are no answers anyway.

I wish it were that simple. Maybe it is in some professions, although I doubt it. But it is clearly not so simple in the ministry. The poinsettias of Christmas will be dead by Good Friday. And I need someone to help me to Easter.

Call

She called to see how I was. She had been in the hospital recently, and we had been in touch occasionally since. But the call was not to inform me of her condition; rather it was to check in on mine. Not that I had been sick or distressed. She just wanted to know how things were going.

I was surprised. Such calls to the pastor are rare. It is one thing for the pastor to inquire of a parishioner how things are going. It is quite another for a parishioner to make the inquiry of the pastor. I was touched.

Mutuality is sometimes missing in churches. You do not inquire how things are going with your lawyer. You use your lawyer only when you need help. Unless you are your lawyer's friend, there is no mutuality. It is the same with your doctor, dentist, accountant, mechanic.

It is different in churches. At least it should be. If it isn't, then it's not quite a church. Not yet. A church by definition is mutual. "If one member is honored," Paul wrote, "all rejoice together; if one member suffers, all suffer together."

We put the names of our ministers on a bulletin board. We have ministers to advertising, banking, homemaking, schooling, and so on. Every church member is listed. Then on another bulletin board we have a map that shows where each of our ministers lives. And on yet another board we have a map of our college-age ministers. This way we are all ministers together. We do not hire one person to do the ministering for us. That person is simply a minister to ministers.

The New Testament refers to all Christians as laity and teaches that each one can have a ministry. In the floor of the infirmary where I went to college are the words, "Non ministrari sed ministrare." They are a quotation in Latin from Jesus: "Not to be ministered unto but to minister." In a church, everyone is a minister to everyone else. It was the practice of the early church and is part of the priesthood of all believers. My friend was my priest with her phone call.

Family

The pastor must beware of trading family in on church-family. One becomes close to a large number of people. Their joys become the pastor's joys. So do their sorrows. Before long the pastor feels pulled between family and church-family. Both need attention. Both are in need day and night. With the pastor's strong Calvinistic work ethic, it is easy to find oneself being pulled away from one's family.

One way out of this dilemma is the Catholic way of celibacy. The priest or nun is married to the church. That eliminates the other-family need. But, as we are seeing, it does not appear to eliminate it fully. There is an increasing drive toward a married clergy in the Catholic church. The old way may have worked for centuries, but in the latter part of this century we are seeing a push toward something new.

Another way out is to view the job with a sense of proportion. Can anything be more important than family? Time must be set aside and regularly kept except for emergencies. One of the foremost preachers of the century, Harry Emerson Fosdick, used to say: "I keep the morning hours absolutely segregated from invasion." That was the time during which he worked on his sermon. Pastors must say the same about their family hours. That means the pulpit committee needs to agree with the pastor from the beginning that, of the twenty-one periods a week—morning, afternoon, evening, seven days—a certain number are to be dedicated to family. That will relieve the Calvinist of any guilt at being away from the job.

The doctor or dentist or lawyer or accountant or mechanic goes home from patients, clients, or customers. The pastor goes home from brothers and sisters in Christ. They are intense competition for sons and daughters and spouse. There is only one way to keep the church-family from winning. It is to cut one's own family into one's schedule with a blowtorch.

Astonishment

I had been in his office half an hour. "I know you have things to do," I said. "I just wanted to stop by and say hello." "No," he said. "I have time. Tell me about your life. What are your goals?" It was virtually unprecedented.

People come to the pastor for help. They have an emotional or spiritual problem. But when the pastor drops in on them, they are not always sure how to act. They have no problem. They want no help. They don't know why the pastor is there.

Curiously, he was suspicious. When I called to set up the time he said, "What are you going to ask me to do?" He thought I was coming to get him to do something for the church. "Nothing," I said. "I just want to come and be with you a few minutes."

Apparently it astonished him that I was not coming to ask for help on a church problem or to offer help on a personal one. *I* was astonished that he was able to see that I was there for us and not for him. We avoided becoming experts and instead became friends. The second half hour we talked about me. I drove back to my office with the radio off.

177

Pedestal

"Nobody comes to me. Jim won't call me back. There's no two-way street. You won't come to me either. But you are my minister. You aren't my friend. Don't get me wrong. . . ."

He feels unappreciated by others in the church. He will gladly talk about his faith with them, but they are reluctant to come to him. I also had not gone to him, but even if I had, it would not have counted. I was his minister, he said, not his friend.

The pedestal-syndrome is a common problem for pastors. It comes from two sources. One is that the pastor is an authority in the work of the ministry. Virtually no layperson has had the training in theology and Scripture that the pastor had in the seminary. When there are other pastors in the congregation, which is rare, there is no pedestal-complex on their part because they have usually had similar training.

The other source of the complex is the congregation's need to have an authority. If it is true that religion deals with life's most vexing questions, then it follows that we need people trained in how to deal with them. A pastor is paid for expertise, the reasoning goes, not for friendship.

Such reasoning is, of course, a fundamental misreading of the pastor's role. One of the pastor's jobs is to befriend, especially those who are friendless. Jesus was "a friend of sinners." The first thing he did was collect twelve people to be his friends. The pedestal-syndrome did not render friendship impossible.

Unfortunately, pastors may abet the complex. They can be remote, pompous, preachy. When my friend said, "You aren't my friend," he forced me to some quick self-examination. What works best for me is to schedule such times for friendship into my day. The demands of the job are such that if calls are not scheduled and appointments made, it is impossible to function as anyone's friend. Realizing that, he and I have set up a time and now meet regularly each week. I will not cease being his minister.

But I will also become his friend. As to why others don't come to him, that's something we will talk about, as friends do. And, as friends do, I will share quandaries from my life with him.

Stereotype

He had just lost his job, and we were talking about possibilities when he said, enviously, "Everything you do is one-hundred percent for good." I hastened to assure him that was a stereotype. The reality of my job was doubtless little different from the reality of his, past or future. But he would have none of it.

There is a widespread phenomenon these days of people in middle age going into the professional ministry. Try as one will to talk about all jobs as ministry, many still view "the minister" as one working solely for good. The danger in such stereotypes is that the pastor is viewed as a step above the average layperson who has to "grub" in "the real world" for a livelihood. If all the pastor does is for good and much that the layperson does is for ill, then we very soon have those who are "close to God" and those who are not. But most pastors will admit that some in the congregation are closer to God than they are.

With this way of thinking we also have pastors who are irrelevant. Nobody can be involved one-hundred percent in doing good. Such stereotypes perpetuate a view of the pastor as holy, which can quickly become holier-than-thou. This explains why many who "have to meet a payroll" and "punch a time clock" write ministers off. I was at a luncheon the other day of some thirty people, all strangers to me, and when in the course of the conversation they discovered I was a minister, they had little more to say. Not a single question was directed my way as to who I was, the nature of my job, my family, my favorite baseball team. It was up to me to carry the conversational ball.

My friend has left his job because his firm was bought by another. It was a job that affected literally hundreds of lives. Prior to that he had had a job which affected thousands. My job is to get him to see his next job as ministry. It is to help him see the possibility of maximum good in what he does, too.

Statistics

It is tempting to become disheartened in a job like this. Of course, it's easy to become disheartened in any job. In the ministry there are few short-term results. There's the same crowd on Sunday morning. The budget inches up each year. The youth group gradually increases. The number of people studying the Bible goes up ever so slightly, the number praying, the number in service projects.

One answer to being disheartened is to say it's in the Lord's hands, which, of course, it is. But such an answer can be a copout. If it's in the Lord's hands, then it's out of my hands, and I don't have to work hard to help the Lord along. One is reminded of the man with the overgrown vacant lot. One day he cleaned it up. A friend dropped by. "My, what a good job you and God have done," the friend said. "Yes," said the man, "but you should have seen it when God had it all to himself."

Another answer is an equal copout. It is to say that "statistics don't mean anything. All that counts is what's happening to a person inside." That's true as far as it goes, but it doesn't go far enough. If something is happening on the inside, it's going to be reflected on the outside. A person making progress in prayer is also going to be praying with other people in hospitals, homes, and church. That's what church is all about. "Faith without works," James wrote, "is dead."

The statistics that matter are the percents, and they are the ones that are slow. A church of 2,400 members may have only

800 worshiping on a given Sunday. A church of 400 may have 200. The second church is more of a church. If corporate growth were as slow as some church growth, management would invest in something else or shake up the troops.

The only way I have ever found to handle pastoral impatience is to be impatient with self and patient with others. That's more than a shibboleth. If the church isn't growing, it may be because the pastor is not growing. Not always, of course, but often, and often enough to be easy on others and hard on self. Not as a masochist, of course, but as a realist. I know a church that is packed every Sunday, and not just in gross figures but in percents. There are many reasons, but one of the reasons is that the pastor is growing. When the growth is in, eventually it will be out. Jesus and the disciples proved that. By the year 313, the entire Roman Empire was Christian. And all from one man with his twelve friends and the women who were with him all along, growing together.

Perfection

"What I liked best was when you blew your lines," she said. We were rehearsing for the choir show. I had been dragooned into a duet with an alto, and I clean missed the better part of a couple of verses.

What she was referring to was the impression people sometimes have that pastors can do no wrong. The sermon is finely honed. The service proceeds without a hitch. The committees run smoothly. Most pastors are in their element, and it shows.

To be sure, a lot of this is projection on the part of the congregation. They need pastors to be at their best. They need good performances. They need the image of a church that is functioning like clockwork.

Still, the flawless image, either projected by the pastor or projected onto the pastor by the people, is a mixed blessing. It is a blessing because one should be held by oneself and one's employers to high performance standards. After all, the church *is* a workplace as well as a love place. But the flawless image is a mixed blessing because flawless performance can alienate flawed human beings. No one can be that good. Fortunately, it is stunningly clear, from time to time, that one isn't.

We were passing the communion one Sunday, and I held up the bread and said, "Let us drink bread together." I can still see the look on one elder's face. It was a mixture of horror and guffaw. I then held up the wine and said, "Let us eat wine together." The whole line of elders cracked up.

When show time came around I had things in pretty good order, but I still flubbed in one place. It was O.K. that I did.

Dilettante

You cannot escape the feeling that a lot of what goes on in churches is dilettantism. A man came up to me the other night at a dinner party and eased me aside to say this, this, and this were wrong with the church. He did not, however, want to get involved in righting the wrongs. He's a sincere parishioner. I'm sure he considered his comments constructive and did not see the inconsistency between them and his indolence.

Ministers can be dilettantes, too. They don't report to anyone monthly. No one is breathing down their necks. They come and go as they please, set their own priorities, call their own shots. A minister can work a forty-hour week and no one would know the difference. Personnel committees function once a quarter at most, and committee members are so busy running their own jobs and homes that they have little time to check on how the minister is running their church.

182

The cure for dilettantism is professionalism. Both clergy and laity are called to view their Christian commitment as full-time, top-priority, and not in sixth place after the Little League and the painting class. The key to doing that is giving people jobs that will expand them. Not jobs but calls. This means that ministers have to know their people, and it means they have to be doing their own jobs first. "An institution is the lengthened shadow of one man," Emerson said. And if that "one person," as we would say today, is a dilettante, watch out. Often the people will be.

My friend's coming up to me at the dinner party is proof that I haven't challenged him with a call. He may be a dilettante because I am. No, that doesn't mean that I am responsible for his behavior. But it does mean that I am responsible for seeing that he is startled out of his complacency. If he is still viewing the church as something that does not merit the investment of his time, then it is my job to be professional enough to move him from criticism to call.

One of the classic bromides in my profession is that ministers are called to be faithful, not to be competent. That is dilettantism.

Youth

Every week two seventh-grade girls give me an enormous hug. After the final day of the eighth-grade confirmation class, I came out to the parking lot to find my car festooned with ribbons and cans and balloons. Senior highs drop in to talk. When students are home from college, some always stop by or call. And every so often a child will thrust something made in Sunday school into my hand.

One of the delights of being with this people, this parish is the way I am kept in touch with my youth. To be sure, my own children do that, but to be in a job in which children and youth are part of the job description is to be kept in touch with an essential part of oneself. Recently, for instance, I had occasion to write a letter to a three-year-old, and not long ago I had a good correspondence about ethics with one of our students abroad. Then there are the innumerable letters of recommendation for summer jobs and college and full-time employment.

Jesus was in the temple at the age of twelve asking his questions. It is the questions from youth that haunt us. Is there a God? Where is the evidence? What makes Jesus important? Is there a need for the church? It is as though all our lives were spent working on answers to our youthful questions. Indeed, our lives may be rewarding to the extent that we feel we have come up with answers.

The temptation, of course, is to let the questions go. After all, one must put the bread on the table, and one does not have the luxury of time to pursue answers. Perhaps. But not in the ministry. The minister is the one in the parish whom the others pay *to* have the time to develop answers to life's deepest questions. Although no longer youths, pastors remind us of the questions of youth. They keep us asking the tough questions.

So when the confirmation class was over and the balloons flew from the doors of my car, I was grateful to my youthful friends for thanking me for listening while they asked their questions. In the same way, of course, God listens to me.

My Clock

My clock sits on the top shelf, obliquely, with its face out to any who enter the room. The hands are at eleven o'clock, as they have been for weeks, months. It isn't that my clock doesn't work or that it's an energy drain or that it's redundant. It is that it is so very much my clock, with an inscription on it from thousands of people representing a movement, an action at one time in my life, that now seems so far removed as to be without energy. I

184

stare back at the listless face and wonder: If that much action is devoid of energy now, in how many such actions am I gradually depleting my life?

Sometimes it seems as though I pulled the plug on my clock as if to transfix a moment in time. It was a good moment. I was running for mayor of Albany, New York. It seemed to be a logical extension of my ministry in a local church. The city was down-at-the-heels. It was run by a political machine. A party functionary confessed at a meeting in our church that, yes, it was true, occasionally they had to "put the peek on people" in the voting booth to see how they voted. So we "took arms against a sea of (urban) troubles and by opposing (did not) end them." We lost. It was a noble attempt, no doubt, but the machine that ruled then rules now, and I am left wondering whether the vast amount of energy expended was worth it.

Perhaps the only way out of such musings is to remind oneself that one does what one must in the moment and leaves the results to God. Maybe that's what faith is. Faith is being agnostic about results. In prayer, for instance, the results are rarely obvious, at least not for some time. Faith is leaving the results to God. Indeed, so much of what happens in churches is not immediately successful. Perhaps church is where we practice not being "results-oriented." Perhaps it is where we do what we must and let God take it from there.

As I look at my clock, I know that something important happened. It may not have been what I wanted to have happen. After all, I lost. But, over the years, things have improved. We elected a congressman, a district attorney, two to the state assembly, one to the state senate. You no longer hear of the "peek." And the assessment racket, in which an alderman would come to your door and offer to get your assessment reduced, is practiced no more. Those are important results, and they came from initial "failure."

We are the sum of what we have done. No matter is lost, the physicists tell us. No energy is wasted—not if we do God's work in God's way and then leave the results to God. Maybe that's who God is. God *is* the one to whom we leave the results. I plug in my clock.

Reality

"I know you're not in touch with reality," he said, half-joking. But it was only half. Pastors get this. They tend to be written off as otherworldly. As a wag once put it, "They can be so heavenly minded that they are of no earthly use."

In fact, pastors are in touch with "the real world" more than most. In any given week a pastor may deal with divorce, drugs, murder, alcoholism, child abuse, suicide. A minister may well be in touch with more "reality" in a week than most people are in a decade.

Or take another commonplace dimension of "the real world"—"the bottom line." Most ministers run small to medium-sized corporations. They are the chief executive officers. It is their job to manage the business, "mind the store," "show a profit" in rising membership and budget. As with any business, if the CEO does not perform, the CEO is fired. One can hardly be more in touch with "reality" than that.

But what is "real"? Surely the psychiatric and economic are aspects of "reality." But there is more. When we limit our definition of reality to this world, we discover that we have a very limited view indeed. It has been said that "realistic" is spelled l-i-m-i-t-e-d. Indeed, the essence of the Christian faith is that the divine dimension of reality invaded the human. That took place in the Incarnation. "He did not count equality with God a thing to be grasped," Paul wrote, "but emptied himself, taking the form of a servant."

Up through the time of Aquinas, the divine dimension was called Reality, with a capital "R." It came from the "realism" of Plato, in whose philosophy the real was what could not be seen, was insubstantial, otherworldly, existed in what he called the world of "forms." The chair on which I sit is real only as it participates in the form of chairness. Later the nominalists, after the time of Aquinas, were to say that the "name" by which the chair was "denominated" was just as real as the reality it represented.

Thus, we need the psychiatrist and executive as well as the pastor. Indeed, it could be argued that the pastor, functioning as both "psychiatrist" and "executive," is in touch with more "reality" than either because the pastor specifically includes the theological as it invades the psychiatric and economic. The pastor's job is to reincarnate the Incarnation. As another wag has put it, the pastor's head may be in the clouds, but the pastor's feet are always on the ground.

Mistake

A job like this gives you plenty of chances to make mistakes. I make my share. Like the time I forgot to tell the committee chair something important that had come up in the committee's area before the board meeting. When I mentioned it at the meeting, the committee and other members of the board were surprised, to say the least.

If I were judged by my mistakes, I would have been out of this job long ago. No doubt one could say that of any job, but what the church offers is a remarkable opportunity to experience grace. Grace is acquitting a person of his or her mistakes. It is clearing the slate. The reason we call grace divine is that mistakes deserve punishment rather than acquittal.

My punishment came in the form of embarrassment. I will not soon forget the flinty gaze of the committee chair, nor the startled looks of the board members. I apologized as best I could. Grace is feeling no need to apologize further. It is the feeling that one can move beyond one's comeuppance into the broad new space of forgiveness. "Father, forgive them, for they know not what they do." Jesus said that as he was being killed. It is undoubtedly the most astonishing example of grace in history.

Its impact was so powerful that it was picked up. Stephen, the first Christian martyr, said essentially the same thing as he was being killed. "Father, do not hold this sin against them." Grace is not holding others' sins against them. We have the opportunity to practice that in a church. Unfortunately, churches are notorious for holding people's sins against them. That is one reason for so many denominations. If you do not experience grace my way, then I do not want to be in the same church with you. If you touch people with water at baptism, for instance, rather than immerse them in water, then we can no longer worship together. It is absurd. More to the point, it is ungracious.

Moving On

Word drifts back that an old friend in a former church has died. It is years since we last saw each other. But we were close when I was there. It is the way of being a pastor. You come, you go. Then suddenly you are back, as with this letter about my friend. He was on the committee that "called" me.

Moving on is perhaps the single hardest thing about the ministry. You get close over the years, and then it is time to move on. One wonders about the sense of that. Why do ministers "have to move on"? Doctors don't. Lawyers don't. Accountants don't. They build up a practice. They stay. It would be economic suicide to go.

We are here now. I see no reason to go. We have been here several years. In many denominations that would mean "time to move on." But such conventional thinking fails to consider the advantages of staying. To be sure, there are disadvantages. One wears out one's welcome with certain people; for some, one begins to abrade. Others feel the congregation needs a fresh face.

But the advantages far outweigh. We are close now. We are a family. One does not break up a family because the pay is better and the challenge greater. The challenge is not necessarily greater. It would take another several years to get this close to another congregation; and if the church were twice the size of this one, it would take twice as long. What is the point?

It takes a while to learn what should be obvious from the start. One does not always know where home is in one's first parish or even one's second. One is looking ahead to the next call. But by the time of the third or fourth parish, one becomes unconventionally wise. These are your people, your parish. This is where you were meant to be. The people on the committee that called you have become some of the most important people in your life.

So when the letter came about my old friend on the old committee, I looked back with affection. He took me to the airplane through the snow. He chaired the committee on worship. He and his wife took us to the ball park. They had us over. Now he is gone. I dropped her a note and thought, "What a paltry thing, a note, to say to her all I could have said to him while I was there." I hope he knew.

A Pastor, Too

Every pastor dreams of such a letter. It came without warning. I was going through the mail one day, and there it was.

We had been out of touch for years. He was in a parish I had served long since, and at the time he had been in grade school. He was writing to tell me that he was about to be ordained and that I was one reason, and a big one.

Every pastor hopes to inspire others to become pastors. "To Timothy, my true child in the faith." Timothy in the New Testament had become a pastor, too. It was a great moment for his mentor. No, I could scarcely be called a mentor for my young friend, but I must somehow have communicated my enthusiasm for my call. I remember how my father, also a pastor, wrote a celebrated sermon called, "The Most Rewarding Work in the World." It influenced countless young people to enter seminary.

Our call as Christians is to make more. "Go," Jesus said, "and make disciples of all nations." There is a built-in evangelism to being a Christian. "How many people have given their lives to Christ because of me?" is a question Christians ask themselves. The answer is not always encouraging.

There is something hopeful, however, in my being used, virtually in spite of myself, to influence a boy. I did not know I was doing it. "Christianity is caught, not taught," is an ancient platitude. But there may be more truth to it than we are wont to admit. Evangelism as a byproduct of who we are as Christians may be more effective than evangelism as a "product" which we "sell."

One must be careful, though. It is easy to use the byproduct route as a dodge. "I won't carry the good news to my neighbors. I'll simply let them watch the way I live." One needs overt as well as covert evangelism. There is a challenge to do the second without being listless.

I wrote my young friend back, welcoming him to the most rewarding work in the world. The generations of Christian pastors continue.

Part of the Family

I was ticking off some of his relative's fine qualities to the college student when I found myself saying, "It runs in the family." "You're part of the family, too," he said.

At another time a woman was telling me what she was going to speak about in church the next Sunday. After we had prayed, she leaned forward and said, "You are a wonderful addition to our family."

There is hardly a pastor anywhere who has not received such gifts. A pastor's family increases geometrically when the pastor takes on a church. But it doesn't happen at once. These two affirmations came long after our arrival here.

The Pastor in This Parish

Finding oneself in another's family, no matter how metaphoric, involves the periodic receiving of such gifts. It can be embarrassing. For one thing, the pastor hardly feels worthy of such intimacies. For another, they seem hyperbolic. And for another, they entail grave responsibilities.

As for the first, of course one isn't worthy. One never is. But that is the point of grace. One is being given a gift regardless of one's worthiness. Grace is unconditional love. If grace were conditional upon our being lovable, there wouldn't be any grace. For the pastor, the family's gift of inclusion is an emblem of God.

As for the second point, what is wrong with hyperbole? Jesus used it often. He talked of the camel going through the eye of the needle. You can't get much more hyperbolic than that. And it may well be that the hyperbole is genuine. Indeed, one must assume it is genuine until it is proved otherwise. Furthermore, it is yet one more instance of God's love being lavished upon us when another family accepts us as one of their own.

As for the third point, what is embarrassing about additional responsibilities in life? Clearly if a member of one's new family were ill, the pastor would be there. Clearly if one had received some honor, the pastor would be there, too. It is analogous to being a friend. Friends are not self-conscious about the responsibilities of friendship.

Why, then, the embarrassment? Because the pastor has not yet fully learned how to receive. "What have you that you did not receive?" Paul asked. In this one sentence, Augustine saw the whole doctrine of grace. God "loadeth us with benefits," the Bible says. God gives us life, health, wealth, family, country, food, job, love. The list is endless. Also endless is our difficulty in accepting, our self-consciousness, our embarrassment. It appears to be part of the human condition.

Maybe that is why Jesus said, "Unless you turn and become like children, you will never enter the kingdom of heaven." A child knows how to receive a gift. No embarrassment there. I mustered a simple "Thank you" to each who had included me.

Twenty-fifth Anniversary

Dear Bob,

I'm sure you don't remember us after so many years. On this date, twenty-five years ago, you married us under the grape arbor at my parents' home. I believe ours was the first wedding you performed after your ordination.

We wanted to write you, on the occasion of our twenty-fifth anniversary, to thank you for starting it all. We also thought you might be gratified to know that the first couple you married is *still* married, and looking forward to the next twenty-five years.

We have five sons, ages sixteen to twenty-four. John is a research physicist. I went to law school and have been practicing now for five years.

We assume that you recently celebrated the twenty-fifth anniversary of your ordination, and we offer our congratulations.

Sincerely,

Epilogue

I thank my God in all my remembrance of you,
always in every prayer of mine for you all
making my prayer with joy,
thankful for your partnership in the gospel
from the first day until now.

Philippians 1:3–5